Also by Suzie Daggett

From Ego to Soul
Discover what your Soul needs... and what your Ego wants

PEARLS ~ 52 Contemplative Insights
Practical Life Advice ~ Timeless Spiritual Wisdom

The Pink Door

Love. Honor Permission. Forgiveness.

Mom's Journey to the Other Side

SUZIE DAGGETT

DEDICATION

To my mom, Lorenita Forster Weisenberg, who always said "Everything you know, you learned at my feet!" And I so appreciate her teaching me.

For life and death are one, even as the river and the sea are one.

~ Khalil Gibran

CHAPTERS

ACKNOWLEDGMENTS

My true gratitude goes to many people who have been instrumental in providing assistance in the creation of **The Pink Door**. Jan Fishler sketched the book outline when I was more than muddled on how to begin. Her content editing followed giving the book the right form. Lisa Schliff's editing skills corrected my many comma mistakes and fixed writing oddities. Jane Marko's eye changed the book for the better.

Therese Wells is a dedicated artist, giving the book cover just the right style and designing the inside structure for easy readability. I cannot imagine what I would do without her eye, ear and soft way to bring excellence to this book and other ventures.

My creative daughter Anna Daggett helped by suggesting language changes in just the right spots and then, with ease and an eye for her mama, took my author photo.

Brent, my husband who stands by me no matter how long a project takes or how "successful" it is or will or won't be deserves a trophy for loving endurance.

The continuous energetic support from my family and friends, especially you helpful beta readers was felt and lovingly received.

And to the most creative comforting team who loved Mom up…John, Sharon, Mo, Nurse Nancy and Annie – Mom and I hold you in our hearts for the kindness you brought to her end of life/beginning of new life process.

Thank you, thank you, thank you to all of you.

ABOUT THIS BOOK

When I run into friends, one of the first questions I ask is "how is your Mom?" We share the same set of circumstances – the care and loving of an aging parent. In our mid 50's to early 70's, our moms or dads are failing. Some are in nursing homes, some still struggling to be independent, some at home with help, some in another state or city, and some live in adjoining housing. Each has problems their adult children are trying to solve, fix or help with.

If this is familiar territory or up-and-coming reality for you, *The Pink Door* will give you a peek into what it is like in the last dying days of an elder: how to cope as a non-professional caregiver; specific helpful ideas to weather rotten moments; the importance of love, permission to pass and forgiveness; and how to live in the moment while loving your elder.

The Pink Door reveals the lessons I learned as I orchestrated the events allowing Mom to pass with peace. She had a plan, she had a destiny, she had an adventure in mind and we were her assistants honoring her timing and needs. Medical intervention was not on the agenda, nor was saving her from passing. Exiting this life with love and permission was her preference.

The Pink Door

1 LEAD IN

About a week before she died, I helped Mom get resettled and cozy in her bed. For a moment, she was her old spirited self, full of life rather than subdued and quiet. Her face and eyes bright with wonder, she mentioned she missed her chance to go through the door.

"*What door,*" I asked?

"*The door to the Other Side.*"

"*What color was it?*"

"*Pink.*"

With clarity, Mom explained the sorrow she felt because three days ago the opportunity to pass through the door was available, and she did not walk through. She felt she had lost her golden opportunity to exit this life with grace and ease. Mom, several weeks from her 91st birthday, had been looking for that elusive door for several years. Suddenly, it was right there, but she did not twist the door handle and walk through.

She was getting progressively weaker, remote and ready to be done with this earthly world. Even with her heart and soul ripe and willing, it just wasn't her time yet. We believe only the Divine knows the timing for anyone's death, yet she still felt bereft at missing her highly desired chance to

1

finally open the door and pass to the Other Side.

I wondered why a pink door until I noticed her cherished collection of pink healing stones on the dresser. Were they calming energetic helpers for the life she was leaving? Did they give her a sense of ease as well as a connection to the Other Side? Or were they just pretty stones? She never elaborated, I did not ask.

I had never seen anyone die. I knew nothing about the dying process and by nature I am not a natural caregiver. The end-of-life passing is mysterious and foreign to me. I had successfully kept the process of helping one die at arm's length. No longer.

As her daughter, neighbor and the 'one in charge', it fell to me to oversee Mom's care. I was unschooled, tentative, confused, impatient and soon to be exhausted. Yet I found myself creating a cushion of love and tenderness to support her. Mom didn't have a specific illness, was not under hospice care and wasn't in the hospital. She was dying of old age at home, in her bed, with family and caregivers who had the privilege of "loving her up."

This is my story of how I negotiated the myriad tangled webs of uncertainty and lack of knowledge as I helped Mom pass to the Other Side. I was edgy and emotional at times, yet I grew as a human and spiritual being watching Mom die on her own terms. I learned many useful elements about the dying process. And I softened in my attitude towards life and death.

2 GATHERING MY STRENGTH

While Mom was dying, I needed to write to keep myself sane. After caring for her, I would walk the 50 steps separating our homes and collapse with gratitude. Within seconds, I got the urge to journal about the day's flow, trails, activities, tears or laughter. With a sigh, I rose from my bed and went to my office computer. Included in this book are my twenty-eight journal entries about the emotional rollercoaster I underwent, insights learned followed by life story narratives, or further tips on the milestones of dying. It is mostly about the respect and honor the caregivers paid to the way Mom wanted and chose to die, rather than how we thought it should be.

All the '*shoulds*' – opinions like: she should be in the hospital, she should get more medical intervention, she should have more vitamins or this or that type of food to pep her up, were left at the door. No one imposed their beliefs or theories of life and death on mom. They were there to love, honor and support her. Each caregiver knew early on that trying to fix or cure Mom was not an option. Each was present with Mom to keep her safe and out of harm's way. Each was willing to allow her to call the time to stop eating and drinking. This was not easy. This is not how it happens in all circumstances or families, yet with foresight, desire and open communication, a death like Mom's can be seen as a journey rather than an ending.

I am not an expert on the death and dying process, just an observer of my situation, as you will be with yours. Even with my limited knowledge of the dying process, I became adept at being Mom's assistant for her changes and finality. You will as well for your own parent.

Mom's final chapter led me deeper into the realm of loving compassion. My fear of the many changes ahead came tumbling down. My resistance to be her death assistant softened; I softened; I slowed down. With sadness, I watched her morph from a vital person to a withered one in less than five weeks.

When someone dear to you is dying, there is no specific roadmap. Your experience will be uniquely yours. There are, however, some similar elements to make the process gentler and kinder, and which I learned and am sharing.

3 OUR STORY BEGINS

The Players

- Mom – Lorenita, Lore, Mamacita (grandmother) who we caregivers loved up in her last weeks
- Suzie – daughter, prime overseer, loyal devoted caregiver
- Brent – Son-in-law, continuing fixer, hand holder, medicine giver, grounding rock
- John – son, who stepped in with his own brand of humor and love
- Sharon – upstairs eyes and ears and friend to Mom for two years
- Mo – a supportive, loving aide who cooked and cleared out spaces
- Annie – a professional, knowable caregiver whose gift was night care
- Nurse Nancy – home health care nurse and provider of information
- Doctor – prime advisor available by phone, text and home visits

Our Tools

We knew Mom's desires. She wanted:

- Little to no pain or discomfort
- To be as peaceful as possible
- No medical intervention if at all possible
- To be home for her transition
- To like all those who cared for her and she did
- That Louie, her cat would find a new home after she was gone and he did
- To pass with as much ease as possible and she did

Extremely important paperwork

- A continuously filled out daily time-line, where each caregiver noted Mom's food, mood, sleep patterns, bowels, medications, ambience, weakness, alertness and other factors we each felt was of value.
- A current DNR (do not resuscitate) signed by her doctor and hung on her refrigerator
- Paperwork filled out at the local mortuary
- A Power of Attorney held by Suzie
- Her will and trust up to date, family treasures designated and ready for distribution
- All bills and household information handled by Suzie
- A budget and money to pay for what was needed

The house set-up

Mom's house was next door to ours, separated by a common space called The Big Room. Her house became caregiver central. Each caregiver would come at the prescribed time to help Mom. A timeline with a date and time was filled out. This proved to be an excellent communication tool. A baby monitor helped Suzie hear next door.

Equipment

We brought in a portable-potty, a hospital bed to replace her king bed, a walker to replace her cane, then finally a wheelchair. Since we were active in Brent's mom's passing, we had gathered enough necessary medical equipment. It was used one more time.

July 7
The Beginning Of The End

During the last 10 years, Mom had so many bladder infections I was no longer fazed by them, but they were definitely a problem for her.

Mom's body was becoming resistant to antibiotics, infections occurred frequently, and there was little we could do to help her. Over the years, every trick from medicine, herbs and cranberry juice was tried to slow down the pace of her urinary tract infections (UTIs), but nothing seemed to work. This is a common situation for elderly women, and Mom really felt "pissed off" each time she was affected by what she called this "irritating, stupid, who knows why God created women the way He did" problem.

In early July, Mom asked me if I had gotten the results from her latest UTI attack. Results? This was news to me. Mom thought she had given me a sample to take to the doctor for analysis, but she hadn't. She was already several days into her UTI before I took one in.

This is where it gets interesting. The results indicated

there was no infection, yet Mom had all the indications of a UTI.

Then, in the early morning hours on one of her many trips to the bathroom, she fell and ended up with a small cut on her head. Fortunately, she had enough presence of mind to push the medical alert button on her bracelet. Soon after, I received a call and raced next door. I determined there was nothing broken, helped her up and got her to the potty. All that came out was a tiny dribble. Poor dear, due to the pressure she felt, she was getting up every twenty minutes for next to nothing. She was completely exhausted and in danger of ending up in the hospital – something neither of us wanted. As a temporary solution, I put the port-a-potty next to her bed.

Because Mom was so weak, the next morning her doctor came to put in a catheter. Immediately, we could see that blood in her urine was the problem, the result of an old bladder not emptying completely. In the ensuing days, Mom was transported by ambulance to the hospital (she was too weak for me to transport her) where a permanent catheter was inserted. From this point on, she got weaker and weaker until she could not walk or stand with ease.

Was this the beginning of the end or would Mom rally and be fine in a week? Were her nine lives coming to an end? Time would tell. Right now her care was manageable.

INSIGHT _____

You might be getting a signal that the end is near. Are you choosing to ignore the obvious? Like me, you probably want life to go on as it has with no interruptions, so ignoring the signals makes sense. The important question to ask yourself is: Can I give up what I want for my elder's needs? At first, I had a hard time with this, but eventually I softened my attitudes and beliefs to care for Mom and to grow as a human being.

_____

4 MOM'S NINE LIVES

When Mom began her final downhill slide, I felt a need to write about my mixed bag of feelings in the face of her passing. She had lived a long, full life and dodged many medical bullets. Yet we thought she would live forever. When she suffered from an odd illness or had her constant bladder infections she became extremely weak. Many times it looked like she would pass. Instead, she rallied. During times of medical stress, she emphatically stated over and over, "enough is enough!"

A few years ago, her doctor found a stenosis (narrowing of a blood vessel) in her small intestine, something that causes the intestine to die, and a situation that was certain to give Mom the grand opportunity to pass. Mom's doctor was very compassionate and straightforward, never fearing the "you are dying" talk. Mom did not want any operations or invasive treatments and she accepted the news with alert, almost happy awareness. Yet, several days into the disease, she self–repaired! Her doctor had never seen anyone accomplish this. A cat with nine lives, Mom was not going to die – at least not then. Was it unfinished spiritual and emotional business lingering in the background or just Divine Timing?

This is a question that has no answers.

July 17
Pee Day

Mom has a catheter, but getting used to it is a challenge for both of us. She still gets up every twenty minutes to use the potty, but then remembers the catheter. This situation has initiated a new level of care. I am the helper, and a rather inadequate one. I find that my ego and my soul are moving in opposite directions.

What my ego wants is to escape the pee and be able to empty the catheter without pee going all over the rug, her shoes, her pants, my feet, or my hands. Since I've had no instructions on how to empty the bag, I have to improvise. I use a towel and get my fumble fingers to hold a plastic container as I maneuver the clip to release the pee. Thank goodness this works.

What my ego wants is to be free from the caregiving role altogether. What my ego wants is to not be stressed in the role I am in. What my ego wants is an easy way out.

What my soul needs is for me to be calm and available to Mom's discomfort. What my soul needs is for me to accept this time and situation. What my soul needs is for me to forgive my whiney outbursts. What my soul needs is for me to guide Mom gently into the next realm when she is ready. What my soul needs is acceptance that her lingering could go on for some time with no relief for either of us. What my soul needs is to feel and be love when I am around her rather than acting abrupt or exhibiting negative energies. From my soul's perspective, these are Mom's teachings. I need to pay attention and learn in this school we call earth.

We are in a strange dance where Mom wants to leave this earth plane, and the way her body is shutting down, I see signs of it happening. Her body is weak, yet her will is iron strong. She is not afraid of dying. That is not an issue. We do not know what the issue is, or why there is a long pause between living and dying. With candor and honesty, we talk about her situation, coming to no conclusion.

For now, I'm an awkward, untrained dancer who is not interested in participating. I want to find her another partner, a new ballroom, a new dress, but the dance is ours to do together. I want her to be peaceful and pain-free like she wants, but I don't know the best way to lead her in this dance of life and death.

INSIGHT _____

When I am confused, I have a conversation with both my ego and my soul to determine which one is in control, which one I am listening to, and who is my decision maker. Even as I pretend to be a "spiritual being" I find my ego in control most of the time. Fear, anger, confusion and distance, all ego traits, are loud and insistent. The love, caring, compassion and acceptance qualities of my soul are quiet. This is the learning process for me, and perhaps for you as well.

_____

5 OUR SPIRITUAL VALUES

To help you better understand this book, I have included some of the beliefs and values that guided Mom's life (and my own) and her eventual transition. Mom died as she lived, surrounded by love, hope, awareness, and a positive attitude. These values serve as a gateway to understanding certain elements of this book.

Your spiritual or religious path may be different from ours. You may embrace some of the following beliefs. Some may be interesting or intriguing; some will be new to you; a few may be part of your life values; or none will be of interest.

- We believe in a higher loving power called God, The Divine, The Universe, Source, Energy of All, Father Sky, Mother Earth, Spirit.
- When we die, we go back to where we came from - a place of vast boundless, endless love, light and energy.
- We are here on this earth to learn specific unique lessons that are reviewed and deepened in the afterlife.
- We live with love, hope, faith, and awareness to make conscious choices for a better life.

- We believe in the simple ceremonies of life, especially saying thank you, smiling, and being grateful for our experiences.
- We feel with our intuitive senses before engaging the intellect.
- Everything is created from Source, starting with the energy fields of our aura and chakras (energy centers) down to our physical body.
- We are eternal souls, and when we return to earth, we take on a temporary human body to learn about love.
- Angels and guides from the other side are always available for inspiration and help when we listen.
- Everything one experiences can be a life lesson.
- And, Mom's favorite saying, "Whatever you do, be happy and content in your own skin."

JULY 19
Mom's Brake Job

This morning while I was preparing Mom's breakfast of hot cereal, fruit, coffee, and pills, she recounted a memory, one she had been telling over and over recently. She does not have Alzheimer's, but some kind of short-term memory loss is occurring. I struggle to be patient and remind myself to take a deep breath. It is time to let Mom talk without judgment.

The story, which I've heard many times: Mom, Dad, my Uncle Jim and Aunt Delores headed to San Diego so the golfers, sans Mom, could play. Mom had Uncle Jim's car and the day to herself. She got in and started driving, but the car hardly moved forward. In spite of the problem, Mom entered the freeway. She stayed in the slow lane and thought about finding a mechanic to "fix this crazy car" that only crawled when she wanted to zoom. Finally, she realized that the brake was engaged the whole time! The car was fine; it was Mom who ignored the obvious.

Careful listening reveals this old story is a metaphor

for Mom's present condition. Mom is losing her ability to control her body, thus the catheter and continued weakness. Her mind has the brake on tight. She does not recognize how applying the brake keeps her in this world, slowing progress rather than moving towards the end. I know she has a choice to let the brake release go – and by 'go,' I mean move to the beauty, peace and love of the Other Side. Her extremely strong, vibrant will is holding her in the slow lane towards her final destiny. Although she has talked for years about letting go, she is unsure how to do it.

Perhaps it's like driving in a foreign country. The street signs are there, but nothing makes sense.

INSIGHT _____

Even though you've heard the same story many times before, instead of rolling your eyes or pretending to listen, this time really pay attention and see if there's a deeper message, like a dream containing symbols and conveying useful information.

_____

6 FAMILY DYNAMICS

As happens in all families with several children, some siblings are more 'in charge' of their parents than others. And, so it was for me.

As the middle child and the one most interested in the family history and Mom's spiritual path, I was the one present for both dad's passing (in an Alzheimer's unit) and Mom's care at home. My husband Brent held my hand all the way.

Mom and I shared an interest in the mystical and 'something other'. While Mom never pushed her beliefs on me, I accepted them because they made sense. As a result, Mom and I journeyed together in both the ordinary world and the unknown metaphysical, spiritual, mystical, sometimes magical world.

In the late 60's, seeking answers to the *Who Am I* question, we read books about inner knowledge, self-awareness, spiritual essence, psychic phenomena, and intuition. We explored the soul's role in this life and the afterlife keeping us curious, open and questioning. Living a life of intention and meaning was our desire. Our soul's needs were as valid as our human needs. Upon our death we believe we will attend soul school learning what is important for our next life if we choose to or need to come back.

JULY 20
Confusion Reigns

Mom gets up early and makes her own breakfast – coffee and burnt toast smeared with butter. Her fondness for burnt toast has set the fire alarm off more than once. I know she's up by the smell wafting across the Big Room to my side.

This morning, I walk in as she is about to pick up Louie's cat bowl to fill with food. She hesitates, unsure of herself. It's a long way to reach the floor and come back up when you are weak, unsteady and uncertain. If Mom insists on taking care of her household needs (as she says she is), including Louie, we may need to feed him on the counter, every cat's dream.

Today Mom says she is not ready to pass. She needs to get her energy up and regain her strength so she can be a "housewife" again. Yet, even thinking about getting up out of the bed or her chair seems to exhaust her. A month ago, even two weeks ago, it was so easy. Even though she was slow and getting slower, she could still take care of her needs. Today her story flipped from wanting to die to wanting to live. In spite of her determination, it takes time for her mind to engage. Past tasks once easy are now difficult. Mom's stubbornness insists she try.

In spite of what she's saying, her mind and body are unwilling to let go of what is familiar. Her mind fixates on the past. She's going through the motions of living, but with confusion and constraints.

For example, pretending to read after lunch, her eyes close and she is asleep. Midday, when I walk in the room, she is slowly making her way to her reading chair in the living room. Reaching for the TV Guide, she searches for something even though she does not watch daytime television. Her reason? This is where the mind starts showing its stubborn streak – she is looking for when *Modern Family* starts tonight. Is this an excuse for not accepting her current reality?

Soon, she is on the couch sound asleep. When on the couch rather than in bed, she believes she is not being lazy. If she stays in the living room, she feels this will help keep her strength up.

From my perspective, she is confused. I allow her the space to try to get better, but I know it's futile. I am her watcher, observer, helper, and when she is ready to talk, her confidante. However, she keeps her own counsel as her mind and spirit struggle for dominance. My job is to be neutral and helpful without judgment. Not an easy task.

INSIGHT _____

> There is a delicate balance between helping and
> interfering when your loved one is changing. If I
> get bossy, Mom gets defensive. If I give her space
> to do what she wants, our day goes better. When
> the dying process begins, it takes time for the
> body, mind and spirit to come into alignment.
> Nothing can be done to speed up or slow this
> down. Respecting the needs and desires of
> someone preparing to pass is of utmost
> importance.

_____

7 BEING A CAREGIVER

Three months before she died, Mom was having trouble walking across the Big Room (the connecting room to our houses) to join us for dinner. Her gait, which had been slowing for months, was now cautious, measured and uneven. Her hurting feet caused her to take each step gingerly. Finally, I started taking dinner over to her until even that changed.

There was no denying the fact that Mom was approaching the end of her journey here on earth, or so it looked.

Oddly, that's when I became resentful and impatient, my compassion at an all time low. I knew I would be the prime caregiver and would give one hundred percent of my time over to her care. Consequently, my life would be on hold.

I do not lean easily towards warm and fuzzy. I am not inclined to ask: How can I take care of you? What can I do for you? What do you need? I don't possess the patience and attentiveness for the details of caregiving. It says so right in my horoscope (which Mom, an astrologer did for me) and in my adventurous enneagram type of 7. I want freedom and variety, not day after day of helping someone – even Mom, whom I loved very much.

Simply put, the idea of being a caregiver is overwhelming. I do not believe I can do it. I shy away from knowing about scientific medical issues, preferring to bring a quick meal to a sick friend or arrange for someone else to do the hands-on care.

JULY 22
She Woke Up!

Surprisingly, Mom woke up this morning with an appetite and renewed amazement for life. The night before she was not hungry and beyond tired wanting to stay in bed, feeling and talking like she was really, really, really ready to pass. As I rubbed her back, she purred like a contented yet pained kitten. She loved every minute of the touch and love given.

A friend skilled in energy work who helps to ease and soften the dying process called to help guide Mom to where she wanted to be – the Other Side. Mom had asked for her and was animated as she chatted about life and her fondness for passing. This lasted as she settled in to listen with concentrated awareness to the guidance and prayers offered. Then, she faded. Mom received the blessings she sought and was content as she napped afterward.

With Mom sleeping, the healer and I talked, both of us feeling Mom would transition in the night. In tears, I called and texted our family to send her healing love. But, as always, Divine Timing is something one cannot figure out. Even when Mom is surrounded by a multitude of angels, especially her favorite guide, Pepe, and the deep love from family, she still was not ready.

Am I ready for her to pass? I am not sure.

I can help her with the many parts of her diminished small life, fixing food, helping her to get up or down, pulling the covers tight to her neck as she likes them, feeding Louie, finding her glasses, emptying her catheter bag, staying in touch with the doctor and family, loving and appreciating her – in short, helping her in whatever way I can.

What makes me grumpy is the constant up and down of Mom either being here on this planet or drifting off to her greatest adventure. This was one month before she passed. In her own way, she was preparing to let go

INSIGHT _____

> It is important to keep your family aware of what is happening with the caveat that the future is completely unknown. At the time, I thought I knew the time frame. No one does. This is an emotional bouncing ball, which is hard to settle. We have no idea what lies ahead. No one ever does. The mysteries of life and death are perplexing.

_____

8 THE FINAL CALL / PERMISSION

About three weeks before Mom died, she called her four grandchildren. She wanted to have the last conversation with them. They in turn wanted to give her permission to pass with love. It was a win-win situation. No one tried to convince her to get well, stay here or work to revive her flagging energy. There was no energy holding her here. She had freedom from everyone to move along when she was ready. The conversations did not last long.

Her granddaughter Anna recalls,

"Her voice was smooth, tranquil and sure of itself. She spoke, 'Honey, I'm so proud of you, of who you are. You make me so happy. I love you with all of my heart.'

Her voice didn't ripple or waver; it spoke as if endowed with godly foresight and confidence. 'Think of me before you go to bed and when you wake in the morning. I'll be with you always.'

In those few words, she told me she was walking towards her death and that she wasn't afraid of it."

Another granddaughter, Teresa, recalls the same energy and words when she talked with Mom. They talked about family, life, love and how proud Teresa was to be her granddaughter and how proud Mom was to be her Mamacita (grandmother). When they finished the conversation, Teresa said she would call in a week or so and Mom replied,

"I may not be here."

Teresa said "if you are there that would be great and if not, that would be all right too because you would then be with Papa John."

They finished with the powerful words...*I love you.*

Mom's children, grandchildren and caregivers gave her the greatest gift one can give: loving permission to die. They said what they wanted and needed to bring Mom closure for this life. Mom received freedom to do what she had desired for so long, to let go with ease, no guilt, no grief.

Giving an elder permission to die is of vital importance to both the one dying and the ones left here to mourn. It gives both parties peace with the fact that their loved one is dying, allowing for the natural process of life to end. Permission allows the elder to let go in peace and tranquility. Necessary feelings, words and love are communicated, bringing openhearted closure to all.

JULY 23
Irritated

I have no idea why I am irritated today. Mom went from total exhaustion and inertia to being able to get her own lunch. Today she said she was fine and able to take care of herself. Why and how the sudden shift? I have been logging 1.5 miles a day scooting from my house to hers for her care and suddenly I am not needed. What is going on? Is this the burst of energy before passing others have written about?

The visiting nurse was here talking about Hospice care and a catheter in the stomach rather than, well, you know where. The nurse also suggested revisiting Mom's pill regime. After consulting with the doctor, we decided to keep Mom on pain reduction pills only.

The interest Mom had for letting go and passing is suddenly gone, vanished into thin air. Today she has a reserve of energy to stay in the here and now. I should feel grateful, but I am not sure what position this puts me in. Should I be vigilant or lax? Do I check on her, let her get her own food, and feed Louie? What about the catheter? Can she now, miraculously empty it herself? I thought I knew what was going on, but I don't.

And I am irritated.

It doesn't make financial sense to hire someone to sit while Mom sleeps, one of my siblings is not able to help, and the other is standing by for me to call. Right now, everything remains on my shoulders.

Why am I so irritated? Is it because I truly believed Mom would go this time, and I am wrong once again? Why is this living/dying such a complex struggle? Why is letting go of this life so darned impossible? I have no answers, just too many questions.

Because Mom is suddenly doing so well, Brent and I are going to take a picnic dinner to the river and enjoy a swim. We decide it would be okay for her to stay alone for a couple of hours – no cell service or way to get ahold of us – and leave her survival to fate.

Around five, as we were getting ready to leave, Mom realized she could not feed Louie, or take care of herself. I quickly took care of her needs and fed Louie. As I did, I felt mollified in a strange way.

My ego wanted and needed to be in control. I was irritated because for a short time, Mom appeared to be back in charge, as she has her whole life. At the same time, perhaps for the first time, I realized how disoriented I was watching her release control.

Mom's transition was causing me to discover more about myself – who I really am when the going gets tough. I am not sure how I will navigate the slippery slopes of Mom's downward spiral – if indeed she is going down this path. My patience is worn thin. Am I being introduced to the values and realities of being a patient soul? We shall see.

When we returned refreshed from the beauty of the

river, I was ready once again to engage in our journey. I found a beautiful piece of prose called "She Let Go" and read it aloud twice, once for Mom and once for me.

SHE LET GO

Without a thought or a word, she let go.
She let go of fear. She let go of judgments.
She let go of the confluence of
opinions swarming around her head.
She let go of the committee of indecision within her.
She let go of all the 'right' reasons.
Wholly and completely, without hesitation or worry,
she just let go.
She didn't ask anyone for advice. She didn't read a
book on how to let go.
She just let go.
She let go of all the memories that held her
back. She let go of all of the
anxiety that kept her from moving forward.
She let go of the planning and all of the calculations
about how to do it just right.
She didn't promise to let go.
She didn't journal about it.
She didn't write the projected date in her Day-
Timer. She made no public announcement.
She didn't check the weather report
or read her daily horoscope.
She just let go.
She didn't analyze whether she should let go.
She didn't call her friends to discuss the matter.
She didn't utter one word.
She just let go.
No one was around when it happened.
There was no applause or congratulations.

No one thanked her or praised her.
No one noticed a thing.
Like a leaf falling from a tree, she just let go.
There was no effort. There was no struggle. It
wasn't good. It wasn't bad.
It was what it was, and it is just that.
In the space of letting go, she let it all be. A small
smile came over her
face. A light breeze blew through her.
And the sun and the moon shone forevermore.
Here's to giving ourselves the gift of letting go...
There's only one guru ~ you.

Author unclear, attributed to the following:
Jennifer Eckert Bernau, Ernest Holmes or Rev. Safire Rose

Today, we need to let go of different things. Mom's need to let go is obvious, but in my case, it's about letting my ego take a flying leap so I can hear my neglected soul, the part of me that is here to learn to graciously and compassionately support and witness Mom's journey, all impatience aside. Sigh!

INSIGHT _____

> *When you find yourself in confusion and impatience as I did, it is important to step away, even for an hour. This refreshes your brain and can switch nervous energy and stubborn impatience to acceptance and awareness of your path. You will be better suited to take care of matters at hand after a necessary break from your new routine.*

> _____

9 THE LETTING GO PROCESS

The idea of letting go and leaving your body is not always as easy as it sounds. Mom thought she could let go at will and instantly be out of her body. But deep in her bones, she was utterly afraid to do it. We openly and frankly discuss what she was feeling. She was surprised at how hard it is to transition. It's one thing to spiritually conceptualize and dream about letting go of what is known and to float with grace towards an unknown dimension, but when the time is near, the body resists mightily.

I reminded Mom that even if her soul and spirit were ready to transition, her body was fighting hard to stay here in this time/space continuum. Her ego remained firmly in control, ignoring the desires of the soul and spirit. As a solution, I suggested she tell her ego, "*Suzie will take good care of you after I am gone.*" She thought that was a clever idea and wondered why she had not thought of it herself! Even at the end, it was still difficult for her to release her body and move forward.

My belief is that the body/mind is the sanctuary for the ego, and without the body, the ego is out of a job. This causes the ego to hold on tight. The ego, afraid and fearful of the unknown future and job displacement, resists by putting the brakes on the letting-go process. This scenario causes one who believes they are ready (like Mom) to fight with tenacity and verve to keep a weak, dying body alive. And fight Mom did, even as she took to her bed and declined both food and water. It was not until she fulfilled her last wishes that she was finally free to let go and be in peace.

When someone is dying yet not ready to release his or her body, it is possible there is an unspoken reason for the struggle. An emotion, memory or forgiveness may need to be spoken or felt to complete the process. This may come out on the last day, last hour, or even in the final minute.

Of course, there are exceptions. Some, like my Aunt Reneé, drop in a chair with no warning. Some linger mute for too many years. Some are too young to die. Sadly, some will suffer without being able to express what's in their hearts. Some will check out not needing to say or do anything. Yet dying consciously or unconsciously happens to all of us. Mom accepted the fact she was dying and looked forward to final peace. In this way, she was a teacher to all around her, especially me.

JULY 24
What are the Ground Rules?

Ever since Mom started her downward spiral, I've been on edge. Is this the day? Will I see her again? Will she wake up? Will her angels carry her to her next wonderful adventure she so often talks about?

Each day she changes, and I have yet to understand if there are ground rules for her exit. What little I understand about the process of dying is that Mom is in the midst of it, but that does little to soothe my intimate experience. I am confused, intimidated and irrational. I like structure and flow rather than the upset and turmoil of not knowing what's coming next.

This morning Mom woke up and wanted coffee at 7:00am, an hour and a half earlier than usual. So, before my coffee, I emptied her catheter bag and took care of her needs.

With concern, she announced, "Louie is missing." Usually, the minute I walk into Mom's side of the house, he starts his plaintive, loud, insistent Siamese meowing. He is hungry all the time, and has a bad habit of eating anything he finds on the counter – butter, bread, left over cereal, bacon grease, potato salad, anything. After searching high and low, finally I spotted him outside the kitchen slider.

Due to poor choices of a former owner, Louie has no front claws, so his outside time is nil to hardly ever, but he is sneaky and strives to get out. Last night he escaped and had an adventure we have yet to unravel.

During the night I heard cats fighting and I suspect Louie was involved. My 18-pound cat, Bo, who was also out all night, is the complete opposite of Louie. Bo lives scared while Louie, barely 6 pounds, believes he owns the property. As the alpha male, he bosses Bo around at every opportunity. Louie came in quite dirty, hungry and tired. Mom, content knowing Louie was fine, finishes her coffee and before I left, she was dozing in her chair.

A few hours later, Mom calls in a panic. "Come quick, quick, Louie is dying." Brent and I race over, but see nothing to indicate his imminent demise. Mom, Brent and I speculate on the possibility the two of them are playing the "who is going first" game. We had an honest laugh when this thought was expressed.

After a morning nap, Mom made her own traditional Sunday breakfast of bacon, egg and toast. She wants to be in charge of living once again. She figured watching a movie in the afternoon will help her regain strength. This is quite different from her normal pattern of reading until dinner. TV was never allowed in our house during the day except for the *Mickey Mouse Club* and *American Bandstand* when my sister and I were young.

Mom's love for reading is changing. She picks up her book and starts to read. Slowly, her eyes close and she is in her quiet world. No longer is her outer world of beauty, curiosity, jewelry, books or food of interest. Her attention focuses on the quiet of her inner world.

I am also changing, matching her pace, no longer

rushing impatiently and imperiously around. My movements are slowing and my speech is calmer as I watch her fade before my eyes.

INSIGHT _____

> *When your elder starts to slowly slip away, note what is happening inside you. Are you full of thoughts and emotions pulling you in every which way? The same is happening for your elder. Breathe deeply as you step back to get a fuller view of the situation. This alone can bring you the strength you need to carry on.*

_____

10 HOW I COPED

Unless you're a professional caregiver, a healthcare expert, or someone who has sat with numerous people who are dying, it's very likely that you'll be unprepared for the experience. At least, that is what I discovered. I will share a few ways I found to help me get through each day and be there for Mom. These coping mechanisms may or may not work for you, but they were of value to me.

My intuition

I have learned to listen and trust my inner voice, which prompts me to do what is required in the moment rather than what is prescribed. Although I was mentally unprepared and sometimes felt I did not have the tools I needed, I did have my intuition, my soul, and open communication with Mom. By using my intuitive skills, I managed to do what was necessary. In retrospect, I believe this helped me navigate Mom's most important moments.

Know what others have experienced

All you have to do is walk into any bookstore or go on-line

to discover a host of excellent books about death and dying. The content of each book is varied. I didn't have the time or desire to read much, so I picked the books that called to me. After reading, I knew a lot more about the dying process from several points of view – from hospice nurses to people who have had near death experiences, dying and coming back. Each journey was unique with common threads that gave me the peace of mind I needed to help Mom. Reading these books helped me to discover what others have experienced and find my way through tears, frustration, and sadness to a place of peace.

Accept that there will be "those days."

There is no right way to be with someone dying, or a right way to die, or a right way to handle your emerging emotions or their physical, emotional, mental and spiritual changes. There is no perfect way to hold the energy for the one who is dying, as you stay present to their needs. We found that if we followed Mom's very subtle prompts and honored her desires to pass to the light, the day went better. If she wanted to eat a hearty breakfast, we made it for her. If she wanted coffee, she got that. We did not impose our ideas of what we thought she must do. She was the leader. Of course, there were bumps in the road, sleepless nights, irritations, bad decision-making, untimely prescriptions, feeling like I was the Lone Ranger lost in the dark woods, frightened I was making mistakes.

Listen, learn and ask for help

Our helper group ranged from kind, nurturing non-professional caregivers to include one well-informed licensed caregiver who knew how to guide us. Along with Mom, they were my teachers, and I followed their lead. I was not afraid to call or text the doctor, nurse or others who had more knowledge than I did.

Write

I started to write the day I knew Mom was on her way through what I now know as her Pink Door. In the process of writing in my journal, I discovered my strengths, delved into my fears, uncovered stories, and transformed my thoughts about life and death. The act of writing helped me solve my issues and confusions around the process.

July 26
Did Other Moms Do This?

Mom had some creative way she lived her life.

My dear friend Linda reminded me of an adventurous moment in the mid-1950's when Mom heard we wanted to be blood sisters. Out of the blue, Mom created a ceremony where under a full moon we sliced open a tiny sliver of skin on our fingers and mixed our blood together. We then let blood drip into a rag and buried it in the back yard with an old penny. We thought this was normal and other kids did rituals like this.

Not until we were older did we understand the preciousness of Mom's character. Where did she get this idea, this knowledge, silly as it may have been? Perhaps it stemmed from her curiosity about all things mystical.

By the late 1960's, Mom began to investigate many avenues of the metaphysical world and became an astrologer. She was remarkably accurate and even today people can remember what she wrote in their horoscope fifty or more years ago. Mom did charts on both my kids when they were two months old, and her intuitive knowledge blended with the stars tells their story. Now that my children are adults, I can affirm that Mom's charts captured their essence and predicted many of the circumstances they have encountered so far in their lives.

When Mom's sister, Fleurette, a nun was dying, she said, "Come on, Lore, tell me when I'm going to die, look at my chart." Mom would not reveal that her sister would most likely die on Thursday of the approaching week, rather than the preferred Wednesday Fleurette ordered up. Fleurette believed she could outwit God and determine her own time to pass. It turned out Mom was right. Fleurette passed on Thursday.

INSIGHT _____

Look to your elder's past to appreciate the changes they are processing. A long-lived life is fodder for storytelling. Sharing family moments, both positive and negative, can bring up stories you have never heard or have forgotten. After your elders are gone, you will have memories to relive.

_____

11 MOM WAS UNUSUAL

Like Mom, I have always felt a bit different from the norm, not following cultural, religious or pop standards. Her strong matriarchal ancestry and spiritual interests took her beyond the linear, logical boxed-in world to a lifestyle that was both fascinating and unique. I followed.

Where did her belief structure come from? Perhaps it was from her strong Spanish/Mexican heritage, mixed with Catholicism and mysticism, new-age ideas, and glimpses into the other side via her psychic abilities. Mom had a near death experience during the birth and death of one child that opened the door to her mystical insight.

She was Rh-negative, making survival hard on both Mom and babies. She carried six babies and lost three. During one birth, Mom started passing into the light (which she loved!) but the doctor pounded on her chest and proclaimed, "You will not die on my table today – think of your children who need you." Boom! Following his instructions, she popped back into her pain body. All her life, she clearly remembered the vibrant bright love on the Other Side with tenderness. She was not afraid of dying. She welcomed the mystery of it all.

Maybe her beliefs were programmed into her DNA,

which I share. Others from her family's cast of characters included healers, psychics and wise women. At a young age, my maternal grandmother had a horoscope written for her – something that was far from mainstream in 1910. My great-aunt was a psychic who was studied by priests and given permission to read as long as she didn't charge. Mom's brother studied and used guided imagery. Her sister, a nun, became a massage therapist in her later years to help the sick. Several cousins on my mom's side were intrigued by the impact of energy healing and the esoteric.

One cousin was thankful to Mom and our grandmother because at age 13, they introduced her to the world of astrology, palmistry, and a touch of mysticism. She recounts: "This allowed me to know and understand myself and others and to help nurture relationships and promote harmony."

JULY 27
Who is the Mom Now?

This morning I ask, "Do you want to lean on me to get out of bed?" Unlike her weakening body, her mind's resistance is deep and strong. She becomes rigid much like a three-year-old only wanting her way. If she could stomp her foot without falling over, she would. Our roles are reversing slowly and surely. I am becoming the mom and Mom is becoming the babe. She needs help with almost everything, yet wants help with nothing.

She walks short distances with slow painful steps assisted by her walker. She can't pee without the catheter. Her hearing is diminishing. Her love of reading is suddenly and sadly gone. Her interest in food and life is getting smaller and smaller. Since most of her dearest family and friends have passed, her interest in others is nil. Being in bed is her new comfort.

Prior to her downturn, she had a great desire to wear lipstick and earrings every day, no matter what. She flaunted her beauty and vanity daily. There are racks and drawers filled with both good and costume jewelry ready for wear. There are fancy and plain clothes in her color range hanging pertly in her closet. She loved and collected shoes! She adored her colorful silver sneakers, popular now, but bought years ago and worn to a frazzle with pride and élan. Now her only concern is comfort, no more shoes not even slippers, just those hospital socks with tracks on the bottom. Her hair is bed hair, her showers infrequent, her daily needs taken care of by others. Her clothes consist of jammies and socks. There is no need for a bra or even undies. This is as simple as it gets. She does not care or notice.

INSIGHT _____

When roles reverse, check in with how you feel about being the one who is in charge, the one your elder relies on. Does it feel uncomfortable? Does it make you feel angry? Are you frustrated? It may be all that and more. Much like a newborn, the dying elderly have distinct needs and desires that only you can fulfill. Doing this with love and compassion rather than resigned duty can switch the energy of the moment and bring deep relief to both of you.

12 MOM BEFORE

Mom carried herself like a queen and everyone who met her, however briefly, remembered her. She was flamboyant, loud, beautiful, striking, full of life and generous with opinions. She had full red lips, big expressive blue eyes and never left the house without her colorful jewelry and lipstick.

As Mom matured, her introspection on living a meaningful life opened the door to three important directions: studying her family's genealogy in depth, becoming an astrologer, and for a while, writing copious poetry when the muse moved her.

The family is grateful for her hours spent tracing our rich background, giving us a firm sense of our heritage. Her knowledge of astrology helped family members with decision-making and finding answers to life's questions. Her intense poetry written in the 1970's was shared with some of the family. Reading it many years later, I wondered what made her heart and soul so vulnerable, so sad and full of deep mysteries.

We never talked about her poetry. I wish we had. (See examples in text and Appendix.)

Mom and Dad had a long and interesting relationship.

They went through a short-term separation, but got back together because, above all, they loved each other. In Mom's words written four years before she died:

"My parents were prominent citizens of Los Angeles during the early twenties. When I married, my parents were against it as my father reminded me my husband was born of a very Germanic family and I from a Latin culture. They were right! But, after 60 years of tremendous upheavals and makeups we decided we had had a wonderful – non-boring relationship. We will continue our battle as soon as I join him. My husband died four years ago, and although I enjoy my life, I am very anxious to join him."

JULY 28
What the Nurse Observed

Nancy, the visiting nurse, came to check on Mom's catheter. We live in a small town and Nancy has helped our family on several occasions. Previously, she tended to Mom for a variety of her health issues, including a broken hip, several bowel obstructions, stenosis (a narrowing) of the lower intestine and gall bladder surgery.

Nancy, kind and helpful, has been a shoulder to lean on. Over the years she has answered endless questions and provided a wealth of important and useful information. We share similar belief systems about life, death, passing and most importantly, the soul's journey.

Today Nancy tells me some of the ways she and the doctor can make Mom more comfortable, whether she is ready to go or interested in staying on this earthly plane. I need her perspective and ideas since I have been operating in a vacuum without necessary skills to make competent decisions.

Is it time to consider hospice? I call the doctor and hospice and find out Mom will not quality for their care. She doesn't have a disease, just old age, which does not fit hospice criteria for six months care.

We are on our own.

This realization makes me feel lost and abandoned as well as let down by the very system designed to help those in the process of passing.

If your elder is dying of old age, you are in limbo, which is where I find myself. I suppose the powers that be want me to help Mom find the closest ice floe and drift peacefully and quietly towards the sunset.

That will not work for Mom, me or anyone else.

Her weight is down to 106, eight pounds less than she was six months ago. She eats like a tiny, disinterested bird and takes a long time doing it. A few months ago, Mom had a swallow test. We discovered that she does not use her back teeth to chew. Since she only uses her front teeth to cut food and chew, her overall chewing ability is greatly diminished. Try this yourself and you will understand how Mom's slow eating is now standard fare. We listen and watch for any eating problems, especially choking, since she seems to cough more now.

It was around this time I knew I needed more help. Sharon, who lives upstairs, had an ongoing caring connection with Mom. I called Mo, who had been with Mom in the past and knew and loved her. Mom was always happy to see Mo, whose lightness of being was an important factor in caring for Mom. My brother John came as needed and our team was ready.

INSIGHT _____

When you are feeling overwhelmed, frustrated, angry, confused, or simply exhausted, it is time to call in the troops. Let friends and family members help you, or if you can afford it, hire the help you need. Be careful thinking you can do it all. This is an ego trap, which is apt to compromise your health. If you're not sure where to go for help, ask your doctor

or nurse, the clergy at your church, your friends.
There are people and agencies ready to help when
you are ready to receive.

_____

13 HOSPICE

When a loved one is dying, you expect help from an organization with knowledge. Hospice is that presumed place. If your loved one has a six-month end-of-life prognosis and is certified by both their physician and the hospice doctor, you may be qualified to receive their fabulous comfort care. Typically, cancer, heart disease, diabetes and other defined medical illnesses are accepted. Their goal is to help and guide you and your family if you choose comfort care over finding a cure. Check with your doctor and the local hospice organization to see if your elder qualifies.

In the case of a natural old-age death like Mom's, hospice is not a fit. Yet, most people will assume you are taken care of by hospice. You are not. Most likely, you are on your own, putting together a rag-tag team of helpers like we did.

August 3
The Yo-yo Factor

Yesterday at bedtime, Mom talked about making the move to the Other Side. Although she was mentally alert, her bones, muscles, blood, and organs were weary. She walked slowly and cautiously. I asked her if she wanted a ride in her walker and the answer was yes. We could get to the bed, chair, or table much faster than when she walked. She was grateful for the ride.

This morning Mom woke up revitalized – ready to partake in her old routine. She sits in her chair where she has sat for the last 30 years. She valiantly tries to read, but her concentration is not keen. Her head bobs and her eyes close. Even though she wants to read, she is soon back in bed for a morning nap. She considers this a failure on her part to stay up and be active. I gently explain she can sleep when she feels the need.

After lunch and a nap, she gets some potato chips from the pantry on her own. I help her to her reading chair and she sits for a short while. Today she is interested in living. Yesterday she was not. What will tomorrow bring? Only the Divine knows and He or She is not talking.

I get aggravated thinking we are heading one direction towards passing only to have Mom do a complete turnaround. Mom says she is feeling okay with staying in her weakened body. I watch this circus in amazement. I need to shut up and remain as non-judgmental as possible. I want to say, "But just yesterday you wanted to go," but I refrain. I need to recognize the strain this has on Mom and me. We do not talk about the stress of it all; instead we carry on according to her needs, desires, and wants.

I try to imagine how hard this process is on people who are suffering with deep unending pain. The patient is miserable and so are the caregivers and families who watch in horror, wondering if they will eventually experience the same when they get close to the end.

I am beginning to see and understand that we are each handed our own brand of suffering. In the end it's what's learned in the process that's important. This goes for the one who is passing and those who love them. My job is to be aware of Mom's process and not let future worries envelope me. I continue to support her as best I can.

INSIGHT _____

When your elder is not sure of whether they want to live or die, they pretend that they can go back to their previous manner of living. To be present with a dying elder, your job, hard as it may be, is to stay neutral to their mood swings. If they want to work to get back their strength, help them. If they want to prepare to pass, help them. This can be an aggravating and confusing time with no specific frame of reference.

_____

14 HEALING ENERGIES

Mom and I appreciated and practiced energy healing. Dad sometimes thought we were nuts, wacky, crazy. His feelings did not hinder us. I recall a family gathering at my uncle's house where my aunt (the nun), my uncle, Mom and I were conducting energy healings on each other and interested guests. Many years later at a funeral, someone came up to me and asked if I still practiced energy work and could I work on her?

During the early 70's, we were with a large group of Mom's healer friends at the beach around a fire for a picnic dinner. This was an unlikely place for a healing, yet Adele, a gifted healer, noticed Dad needed her touch. For five minutes, Adele did her healing work, and dad's pain was gone. He had no reference for this type of healing experience. It stunned and changed him profoundly for the better. He began to understand and accept what Mom and I were studying.

AUGUST 4
A Reading by a Medium

My friend Brian is a medium. He receives information from family and friends on the Other Side and communicates it to those on this side. Upon hearing about Mom, he felt compelled and asked to read for her. Of course, she was interested—as she always is in valued mystical information.

Brian's reading was pretty darned accurate. He picked up on specific incidents and personality traits of my mom's parents, her sister, and my dad. The music of Frank Sinatra showed up. The fact that when my grandfather left the family, he was unable to be with and honor Mom's sadness about not having her dad was spoken. The idea that Mom was my dad's teacher in this life was also mentioned.

Remember, this is a psychic medium reading, not your ordinary conversation of death or about those who have passed. Brian also recounted that Mom's sister, who became a nun at sixteen, was overwhelmed by Mom's free spirit, and joined the Church to obtain the structure she needed.

I knew some of the facts Brian relayed and was

amazed by his accuracy—especially information about my grandmother. The fact that my grandmother had people help her with the kids when they were little had a long-term effect on Mom. Because her mother wasn't emotionally available, Mom turned to the family help, Tomasa or Sadie, for comfort and tenderness. Although they were kind and loving, Mom longed for time with her mother, and she still carried the pain in her heart.

During the reading, Mom received and recognized her mother's love and was able to let go of her inner child's feeling of lack. She needed to know her mother saw her for whom she was as a young woman and loves her for being who she is now.

As a result of the reading, Mom was on the all-important track to forgiveness. Not only did she forgive her mother, but she also forgave herself for what she felt she did wrong in life. After years of being hard on herself, Mom was able to forgive the idea she had done wrong.

The reading lasted less than 45 minutes and brought both Mom and me great comfort. Everything Brian said made perfect sense to Mom, who was grateful for the peek into the mysterious world of communications from loved ones who have passed. I gratefully watched her receive the love, acceptance, and tenderness from her family.

INSIGHT _____

A reading from a medium was of great value to Mom and me, bringing us peace and clarity. This was our home ground, and it felt right as we listened, absorbed and learned. This may be something you wish to do, but first check with others who have experienced this type of psychic reading – it is not for everyone.

_____

15 WE LOVED TO EXPLORE

Because Mom and I had studied in the metaphysical arena, we were very open to information given by qualified psychics, astrologers (Mom) tarot readers, intuitives (me) those who read hands or past life experiences, mediums and more. I remember a time when I was in high school, and Mom and I were at a street fair. We approached a booth where a psychic reader told me one memorable thing.... I was going to be a writer! At the time, I thought she was wacky. It took me a long time to start writing. The timing for what a reader sees or perceives is not in our linear time frame. It happens when the time is ripe.

We also played the Ouija board, asking oddball questions. One night, Mom and I had our fingers on the board asking who was there. The name spelled 'Jesus' – that was enough to spook me. I banished Ouija from my life. Mom was not troubled one bit, and she continued to play the game with my aunts who loved it.

AUGUST 6-10
Brent's Birthday Break

With caregivers in place, we left town to celebrate Brent's birthday. This was the first time he and I had been away since Mom started her final journey. John, Sharon and Mo were confident they could handle whatever came up, so we left for a mini vacation at the beach.

Mom's catheter was changed the day before we left. Unbeknownst to me at the time, the nurse did not secure the bag to her leg. Apparently, securing it to the leg is optional (this was news to us). But in Mom's case, the dangling hose was uncomfortable, disconcerting and irritating. Sharon applied caster oil to relieve the soreness, but it took time to work. Mom started a new regime of twisting and turning, needing to lie down, needing to get up, needing to pee, over and over. She forgot about the catheter and that she could just let her pee flow.

After a sleepless night for Mom and Sharon, the team decided to fill me in on the developments. They called for advice. In spite of sketchy cell service, emails, texting, messaging and phone calls, I got regular updates. The upshot was that everyone was exhausted and Mom confused. I vacillated between relief that I was off duty to guilt about being away and unable to help. When I returned home, I made several calls to fix the catheter issue. Mom and the team were relieved.

The situation made me realize that we caregivers all love Mom and care for her, providing good food, comfy bedding, a positive, loving, kind state of mind, home remedies, prayers and lots and lots of back rubs. However, none of us are nurses, professional caregivers or even close. We are shooting in the dark here, with no knowledge of what we are doing, other than good intentions and our intuition. We keep doing what we can with input here and there from Mom's doctor and the visiting nurse. Is this how everyone operates?

INSIGHT _____

If you have the luxury to get away, it can make all the difference for what is to come. A new perspective can bring new ideas. The end-of-life dance is open-ended, full of challenges and surprises. When you are rested, it's easier to handle life and death.

_____

16 SELF CARE

I am a big believer in self care. I am not one to suffer lightly. I need my sleep, I need my space to recuperate, and I need space to just be. This may sound selfish, but when I don't take care of myself, I cannot care for others. Wandering the empty spaces of the beach was a relieving antidote to caregiving.

While walking alone, I asked the Universe for a special heart rock for Mom. Within a few minutes, there it lay – all alone, a perfect heart shape, just waiting for my eyes to find it. I gave great gratitude for the symbolism delivered by my angels, the Universe or whoever is listening. I am a firm believer in asking, letting go, and receiving. Finding the rock is visible evidence of the mysteries of life.

After we arrived home, Mom received her new heart rock. The simple beauty of the rock shaped by the ocean touched her heart and soul. Instead of beach gray, she wanted it shiny. A quick application of lacquer gave the stone the sheen she desired.

AUGUST 11
Is the End Near?

Mom is so weak, so very weak.

She sleeps most hours during the day and night. The tiny amount of food she eats consists of small bites, which quickly fill her up. She needs help walking. We replaced the walker with a wheelchair. She falls asleep while eating. We need to watch her carefully and sometimes feed her. It may be time for a bland, liquid diet rather than food with texture that she needs to chew. Her spirit seems to be elsewhere as she speaks little or only interacts with short sentences. Her gaze is different, more inward than out. Books and magazines no longer interest her. She enjoys some music, mainly Mozart and a CD of my daughter playing the harp. Mostly Mom likes it to be quiet.

When I ask Mom if she is suffering, her answer is always no.

I am the one who is suffering. The mom I love is fading fast. She droops over, cannot stand on her own, and prefers not to talk. She is shriveled, and it's difficult to watch the decline. I need to find a way to tune into her soul. She has gone from a proud eagle to a broken-down sparrow.

We switch her king-sized bed for a hospital bed that had previously been used by Brent's mother. I find a cute comforter that Mom likes and her room is transformed. Mom, not a big fan of change, seems to readily accept her new bed. This set-up is easier on everyone. The bed is more comfortable for Mom and our backs welcome the change.

She loves to hear thoughts like: *Let Go and Let God.* Softly she says, "That's an oldie but goodie," showing us her mind works. Her bones protrude through her jammies, and moving her requires a soft, gentle touch. I am rough around the edges and tend to move too fast rather than slowly and considerately. In helping her to bed, I accidentally hit her very tender left foot. Ouch! My inner-guidance says to slow down, slow down, Slow Down! I need to match Mom's pace.

One of the caregivers believes the end is close. Who knows? How can we tell? We are floundering here without support. Mom does not qualify for hospice care, but the hospice booklet is very useful. Mom's doctor helps us when we ask, but we are not in control of the timing.

It is Mom's journey and she is leading us.

INSIGHT _____

It's important to realize that the shift from wanting to live and choosing to die is not always obvious and may catch you by surprise. Are they still interested in eating? Watch their sleeping habits. Are they in bed most of the day and night? Are they losing weight? Has their routine changed? Be responsive to their needs and aware of any changes. Use your timeline to track what is different.

_____

17 LIVING & DYING WELL

Mom has an admirable attitude towards both life and death. Her thoughts about passing, letting go, mortality, end of life, eternal rest, the grim reaper, and finality of this earth life allowed those around her to assist her in her last moments with ease rather than pity or misgivings.

With her long-range spiritual view, she shows us how our souls, hearts and beliefs lead us towards eternal love. Her inner light shines with a certainty that all is fine as it is. And we believe her, which betters our lives. She died as she lived – with purpose, out-of-the-box thinking, a pervasive positive attitude of que' sera' sera' - whatever will be will be.

AUGUST 12
A Caregiver's Knowledge

Yesterday, Jill, who helped shower Mom, stopped by for a quick visit. Upon leaving, she gave me a deep hug and said, "It won't be long now."

"What does that mean," I asked?

Jill smiled lovingly and repeated, "It won't be long."

I heard that same fateful phrase when Dad passed in an Alzheimer's unit. I asked the nurse, "How long will it be before he passes, how do you know he is going?" There was no answer, of course. Hospice workers, nurses and others who have witnessed life's ending have an inner knowing that I lack. I have never been around someone who is actively dying.

Dad died five hours after I expressed gratitude and love for what he brought to my life. He was on oxygen and morphine, in a coma, curled up like a newborn with old, old features.

Mom's process is different from Dad's. She's in her bed, at home with her cat Louie, surrounded by loving caregivers. Every moment, we do what we feel is best for her.

Knowing the time for Mom's passing is soon, her doctor suggests letting her decide what and how much to eat and drink. She tells us to give Mom little sips of water if she likes. Eventually, Mom will dehydrate. This will force her kidneys to fail. Perhaps she'll take a final breath before that happens.

This scientifically brutal advice is uncharted, foreign, and emotional territory. There is no softness around the edges, just matter-of-fact failure of the kidneys, then the heart stopping. I had no idea I would feel so disjointed and unsettled.

Brent is a rock keeping me grounded and Mom acknowledges the pain for both of us in her eyes and the few words she speaks. Knowing there is deep love between us is vitally important. I keep letting her know how much I love her, and she nods in agreement, indicating she feels the same way.

Last night Mom only ate a few bites of fruit for dinner. She asked me to feed her. Mom asking for help is a new situation. Suddenly, roles were fully reversed. I tenderly assisted her with tiny bites, reminding her to chew. I patiently waited as she dozed off between bites.

Even though she weighed 98 pounds, she was dead weight and she couldn't always remember what her feet were for, or how to move. I struggled to get her back to bed. I had her situated precariously between the wheelchair and bed while wondering how I was I going to do this alone. Finally, with soft, kind encouragement, she got her left foot to move a tiny bit, then her right until we were able to get her bottom parallel to the bed. With more encouragement, she was able to sit. From there, it got easier. I picked up her legs, which felt like wood, placed them on the bed, put my hands under her bottom, and scooted her back and sideways so she faced the window. Assuring her that she wasn't falling, I slowly placed her head on the pillow and her arms began to relax. Her body was getting rigid and stiff. Moving was difficult for her.

Through my work with the ego and the soul I understand Mom is physically holding on to her body because her ego is fearful. This is part of the letting go process. Her body needs to give the signal to let go, so that her spirit and soul can soar. When Mom dies, her ego will no longer have to protect her.

INSIGHT _____

> *When you come face to face with the inevitable, take time to mourn, cry and grieve to release your pent up emotions. Feel into your heart and let the sadness emerge. By releasing your deep-felt emotions, you are helping yourself and the one passing. Breathe deeply as you process this change in life.*

_____

18 DEATH & DYING

Death can be a hushed-up swept-up under the carpet subject not easily talked about with family members. This is not true in our family. We are open and accepting because we believe that when we die, we go from our finite earth body back to our infinite soul – a place some call Heaven, Nirvana, the Promised Land or the Other Side. Our beliefs allowed us to face the fact Mom was dying with simple truth and love. Doing this together kept us in a circle of healing rather than isolated sadness and grief.

Many families brush their emotions under the table, preferring not to show or know what they are feeling. They may not know how to allow emotions to surface. Left alone, emotions may fester until one brave family member brings up the 'what do we do about Mom' talk. The family may need to make many hard decisions both with Mom and on their own. Including your elder in the discussion of their dying process is a potent conversation to have (if they are able to talk/think).

Questions to consider are: what do they feel happens after their last breath; do they have any people or events to forgive, do they want to live even with a limited body and/or mind, do they desire to pass or be fixed, how do they think they might die and what is important to them. These are very hard questions and some may not be relevant. Your family may need the help and guidance of an experienced gentle professional.

If talking about death and dying is taboo or difficult, the stress level will spike when this insistent elephant in the room is ignored. Instead of fearing the reality of death, consider embracing death as you do birth – a truly magical moment. Just as no two births are exactly alike, there is no typical way to die. Yet, there are similar threads, which can surface during one's passing. Those who fear dying or have people around them fearing death as an absolute ending may be confused about what comes after the release of their last breath.

There are no absolutes, no way to know what will happen. It may depend on what one believes will happen to them. Having courage to gently talk about death can relieve pain and confusion for the elder. Let them speak their mind over time with small steps and compassionate encouragement. Soothing those who are dying takes loving, caring and sharing of this life-changing experience.

AUGUST 12
Do a Reneé

My mom's cousin and best friend since childhood died before she did. Mom was both sad and mad. Sad, because she lost her valued friend, mad because Reneé beat her to the Other Side. My aunt had some physical hardships, which never prevented her from living life fully. She was also a very structured, frugal, and sometimes an inflexible person. And we loved her because she was able to easily laugh at herself and love life.

Like my parents, she and my uncle adored dancing to Frank Sinatra. There are wild, wild stories of my parents and aunt and uncle dancing until early dawn at a local country club, stealing the mascot and riding home on the hood of the car. Whenever I hear these stories, I am amazed they didn't get into trouble. The four of them often traveled together and lived long enough to love each other deeply and sincerely.

My aunt passed the same way her dad did. She was with my uncle and friends enjoying a glass of wine. Suddenly without notice, warning, or a peep, she fell over into the table. She died instantly. We call that "doing a Reneé." Fast, easy, no pain, no words. She simply keeled over after a lively evening out. Mom was envious.

Mom and I giggled about how she too could "do a Reneé." She liked the idea, as it is so simple. However, I don't think that's Mom's way. She is floating between worlds, enjoying both for the moment. We know she will let her breath go and forget to retrieve another at the right time. She says she is ready. I know I am ready and everyone else in the family is ready too. We are patient with the process and do not want her to suffer.

INSIGHT _____

The way an individual dies is not predictable. Some people quietly slip away and others resist until they take their last breath. Whatever is going on, it's important to accept what is happening and be present as an observer. At the same time, don't be afraid to share your feelings or let your loved one know they have permission to go whenever they are ready. Let them know they are loved and will be missed, but you will be fine without them.

_____

Mom's poem about Reneé

6-30-67

Perhaps it's because
    we are kith and kin
no questions or dissections
no advice or reprimands
    posturing's or pose
      missed
    bravado and brass noted
or perhaps because
    we shared life's darkness
    distrust replacing innocence
    preferring armor and moat
    to open arms and heart
or perhaps
    ancient Druid, Celt or Mayan
    laugh at that which
    they spawned
seeing
    superstitious fears
    mystic musings
    hedonistic happenings
Cry and understand
Perhaps this is why
    I call you friend, Reneé

19 BELIEFS AROUND DYING

The beliefs your elder holds in their heart about dying is their unique experience, as Mom's was and mine will be. For example: they may have an image of floating to the clouds to be met by a loved relative or angels; or going through a light-filled tunnel; or passing through the Pearly Gates; or discussing their life with Saint Peter, or just nothingness. It is their journey, and you will have yours.

Mom's beliefs were set early in her life, and she was intrigued by her next journey. Her fear level was low, allowing mine to follow.

I believe her investigation of the spiritual world mixed with her bon vivant manner of living was her path to a gracious passing. Does that mean it was all roses and sweetness? Not at all, yet the temperament and energy around her allowed a frictionless atmosphere. Each caregiver had an affinity with Mom. They appreciated her style, her smile, her openness, her humor, her easy take on life. They flowed with the difficult moments when Mom was in the parallel world of earth and infinity and was unstable.

How someone dies may be a reflection of how they lived, how you relate to them, how long the process is, and how equipped you are to shoulder the good, bad and odd baggage. No matter how wonderful your elder is, how close you are or have been, how much you love them, how many elements of surprise show up, there is always another bag of unknown "stuff" to unwrap and bring to light. Your stuff may be easy or hard to deal with or acknowledge. For the most part, it will appear if it needs to.

This is all part of the growing and learning process that a death in the family imparts. We have our own learned, taught or felt ways to be with the dying, processing a death, and being in peace.

AUGUST 13
She Sat on the Floor

In the wee hours this morning, my intuitive senses woke me. I felt Mom needed me.

I found her sitting on the floor facing her bed. This was a first. My guess is that she tried to stand up by holding onto the bed and nightstand, but her weak legs did not support her the way her strong, intractable mind wanted them too. Slowly and softly without injury, she fell. She did not push her alert button, so I have no idea how long she had been sitting there, nor did she. It could have been hours or minutes.

This was just one of many times in my life where trusting my intuitive senses was important. I helped her back to the comfort of her bed.

Mo came for the morning shift, and Mom asked for hearty breakfast. This was a change since she had not eaten much for days. Mo happily prepared burnt toast with an egg, a fig, and watermelon, plus a small dose of weak coffee.

Mom was quite restless and agitated in the morning. A friend says this part of the dying process is called terminal agitation. Mom had been up and down at least five times in an hour to sit or stand. When she stands, I hold her under her arms and pull her gently to my body. It's an opportunity for a big, juicy, heartfelt hug.

Mom likes it when I stay by her bedside and rub her head, shoulders, back, arms and legs to sooth her and settle her energy. Today we searched for ways to allow her body to let go. Together, we came up with this prayer:

I release my body, which has served me so well.
I thank you my marvelous vessel, my helpful body. You
have been so good to me, and now,
I do not need you any longer.
Do not be afraid, Suzie will take care of you.
I open my crown chakra allowing my spirit
and soul to soar towards the light
and be the beauty of light and love.
I embrace this moment to let my body go and be with
the love of all creation.

Later, Brent and I helped Mom into her wheelchair for a jaunt outside. It was a glorious sunny day, so I put a saucy colorful hat on her. For the first time in a month, she ventured out of her room. The warmth embraced her and with a smile, she viewed every inch of the yard, trees, end of summer weeds, and flowers. Mom said that she liked the energy of being with mama earth. Mom always saw beauty around her.

INSIGHT _____

Reading a favorite passage, prayer or poem is a wonderful way to connect and honor your loved one. If they love the Bible or another religious text, ask if there is a verse that they would like you to read. Make up a prayer as we did. Towards the end of life, your time together can bring a tremendous amount of comfort to both of you.

_____

20 LISTENING

Mom was a good listener when I was growing up. When I was 13, I was French-kissed at a Catholic carnival. This was a first kiss for me, and I was sure I was pregnant. I tearfully told mom the story that night and instead of laughing out loud, which I could see she wanted to, she listened and patiently explained life.

This odd incident taught me about listening. For the last six years at our nightly dinners, Brent and I heard many repeat stories from Mom. We listened with a slight glaze but also respected her story as she did with me many years prior.

At the very end of life, listening to the needs, wants and fears of an elder can be stressful. There are moments you want to interject what is on your mind or just leave the room. It is up to you to support them, be patient, listen, respond, and stay out of judgment.

This is a gift to both of you.

AUGUST 13 (evening)
Roommates

Last night and early this morning, Mom was up twice trying to turn over. She was weak and a fall risk, so we were watchful. We do not want Mom to wind up in the hospital. At midnight, I heard odd noises on the monitor and came over to find Brent sweetly assisting Mom. His intuitive senses led him out of his warm bed to her bedside.

She now needs us day and night.

When she wants to turn over, Mom somehow has the strength to push herself up and swing her legs over the edge of the bed to sit. Exhausted by the effort, she often falls back to sleep, sitting and swaying with her eyes closed. It is getting very hard for her to move her legs, except when no one is around and she is determined to move. She relies on us to lift her legs, put a pillow in between her bony knees, support her head and shoulders as we lie her down, and then gently shift her hips to face one way or another.

Even though it's warm, even hot in the house, Mom is

cold. Brent arranges the covers around her neck for warmth.

To keep an eye on her and protect her from falling, I sleep in her room for the reminder of the night. It's clear that Mom can no longer be alone. I found a twin mattress and put it where the night caregiver could watch her. Her room is ready for day and night care.

This arrangement distresses Mom. She does not want to bother us and doesn't understand that we choose to be with her out of love, concern, and the deep respect we have for her end-of-life process. This does not mollify her.

Mom attempts to control the situation and I'm not giving in.

Mom loves the idea of letting go and being done with this life. Every night for years she has asked her personal guide, Pepe, to help her with this transition. She says: "I am ready. Take me."

So far, her wish has not come true, but soon it will.

INSIGHT _____

The need for 24/7 care can occur at any time. It is another obstacle on the road that once crossed, is rarely reversed. Taking control of your elders' situation can be difficult and sad, but it must be done. This is where managing the situation with courage, strength and love is essential.

_____

21 CONTROL

When an elder is dying, you become the decision maker, the one to guide them as they journey to the end. This is much like when you were born, and your mom and dad feed and clothed you, making all decisions. You could not ask for what you needed, so you used crying or smiling to reach out. Now you are in control of the many moving parts of your elder's life.

Even if Mom did not want to bother me or was distressed, I am sleeping in her room to be sure she was safe. It is my time to be in control. We are two strong women, and control is and has been a tug of war. No longer is Mom strong enough to be the final authority.

She was a decisive person her whole life, never daunted by authority or convention. Once a neighbor called Mom to say she might call the cops if the grandkids did not quiet down. Mom replied, they are safe and happy here, let them have their fun. The neighbor backed down.

AUGUST 14 (evening)
I Give Up

Much to Mom's dismay, I spend a second night in her room. After a few calm hours, the agitation and drama start. Mom is up almost every hour, feeling the need to pee (forgetting she has the catheter), or a desperate need to change directions in bed. When she gets up, I get up. She sits on the side of the bed swaying a bit as she closes her eyes and seems to sleep sitting up. Needless to say, each of our sleep patterns has been greatly disrupted.

In the middle of the night, she is determined to get up and walk on her own. She yells at me (a first) to stay in bed. She does not want to bother me. She uses her imperious Mom voice commanding me, "Suzie go back to bed, NOW! I do not want you helping."

Wow, I did not see that emotional curve ball coming. Remembering that commanding voice from my youth, I shrink inside like a naughty child and retreat to my mattress.

From my vantage point, I watch Mom struggle to find

the energy to get her feet to the floor and attempt to stand. Time after time, she failed. This is repeated into the wee morning hours. No longer can Mom get up, get going, and be a housewife.

Several times she sighs and says, "I give up." Has she really has given up, or is she is talking to her hurt ego? I think she is desperately holding onto a well-developed strong sense of self. Her soul wants to soar, but her ego, so worried it will be out of a job, keeps placing thoughts in her mind like: "Come on Lore, you can do it – just stand up and walk; go to the kitchen and make breakfast; I know you can do it, just try harder."

Her body is so weak that it's very difficult for me to watch this parade of human emotional wants and desires play out. It occurs to me that perhaps Mom has entered into the world of hallucinations or dementia. An expert needs to lead the way with this, not me, the wounded little girl.

I do know I am confused by Mom's wild mood swings, which I know are part of the end-of-life process. Living with them moment-by-moment is vastly different from reading about them. According to a retired hospice nurse, Mom might qualify for help through the hospice Transitions program, but I know better. Mom does not qualify and will not unless she develops a disease that has a six-month end-of-life prognosis.

In the morning, Mo does a magnificent job of feeding Mom, changing her, and helping her up and down (6 times per hour). She even gives Mom rides in the wheelchair. While I am over the top exhausted, Mom looks refreshed as she smiles with Mo.

For me, it's time for a nap.

INSIGHT _____

> *The strange world of emotional stress is apparent when the person we are caring for tries to reverse time and be in control. Sadly, there is no control for them when the next step is death. Even if they are secure with the idea of going, the mind still plays a heavy hand. By being compassionate and loving, caregivers can soften these moments of angst, by actively listening with tenderness and promoting a sense of safety and security.*

_____

22 OLD MEMORIES

When we were kids, our young parents loved to party with friends. There were no babysitters; all the kids were grouped together and we created memorable fun. For the adults, the cocktails flowed while they laughed and danced. At the beginning of a party, Mom always said in her firm voice... *do not bother us unless you are dying.* And we did not until one time when I was 13. My friend and I were fooling around. We would shimmy up a wall with a sink opposite to see how high we could get. I was jostled and came crashing down, landing awkwardly on my left arm, which broke. I sent my friend into the party scene with the news that someone needed to come see me. My mom marched in and said, "If you are going to complain about a headache..." and I replied, "I think I broke my arm."

When an elder reverts to an old personality pattern from your youth, you do also. This can feel awkward and restrictive. Having an awareness of what they are going through internally can help damper the forgotten memories they bring forth.

AUGUST 15
Finding Annie

I feel I am on my own, floating in no woman's land not knowing what to do, whom to call, how to negotiate the rocky road of unknown hazards that lay ahead. I don't know what to expect at this juncture. Do we have one day left? One week? A month or a year?

I calculated the costs for 24-hour care for a year just in case. Ouch! This is costly, but when it comes to Mom's care, I am a hawk. Keeping her at home under my watch is the only option I choose to have. The caregivers on our team have previously cared for Mom. We are a viable team, but we're not nurses or professional caregivers. We surround her with love and devotion, but we need help. I ask the Universe to send an angel.

Annie came to me via a circular set of circumstances, which only the Divine can orchestrate. I volunteer at a used bookstore supporting a neuter/spay clinic for animals. I was doing my shift, a needed break from caregiving, when a retired nurse wandered in looking for an interesting read. We chatted and I shared Mom's situation. The retired nurse knew the right person for the evening shift. Later that day, Annie, a professional caregiver, came to meet Mom, who liked her very much. Annie returned that evening for work. It just turned out she had an open week for night caregiving, her specialty.

What a relief to find respite from the distress and exhaustion I'd been experiencing. Annie was the perfect person for the evening care. She arrived just when it was apparent I could not do another evening without making myself sick.

Mom and I believed in the loving kindness of the Universe and Annie was proof. And she was a charming spiritual person to boot.

INSIGHT _____

It is vital to notice when you have reached your limit and it is time to bring in more help. If you believe in receiving from the Universe, use your prayers to ask for what you need. Listen and watch for the unexpected to come your way. A magical moment can appear if you are open to receiving and believing there is someone just waiting to help.

_____

Mom's poem about truth

11-6-67

And truth –
    what can one say of truth
    when looked at
  dissected
  digested
Even the strong feel soul cringing
and the spirit crying out
  in its weakness
and beg for the return of
  tinted glasses
  colored tissues
  soft cushions.
So truth buckles the knees
of her victims
mashing them into
    formless
    weightless
    masses
  of quavering jelly
But the light of truth
is a scathing
    stunning beacon
to grasp
and hold on too tightly
    for in the end
    that's all that's left
  only truth

23 SPIRITUAL QUERY

Mom and I attended a myriad of metaphysical classes introducing us to the deeper mysteries of life. We knew there were no absolute answers, no complete unwavering truth, yet we felt getting educated in the mystical might bring us a deeper understanding of life and death. And it did.

For eight years, I produced events with well known and newly emerging thought leaders. Mom was always interested and curious, no matter the subject. As she got older, she could not sit through a whole evening. Brent or a friend brought her home early.

I also authored two inspirational wisdom-based books. When Mom read them, she was all smiles and awed by what I had written. Then she said with a giggle and broad smile, "Oh yes, you learned it all at your mother's knee!" She loved taking credit for what I produced, and I loved giving it to her.

AUGUST 16
The Pink Door

Mom continued to be extremely restless last night and today. We were pooped from helping her lie down and get all cozy under the blanket only to get the urge to sit, then stand, then get into the wheelchair to go the living room, then immediately, want to get back in bed – all within 10 minutes.

Over and over and over.

In an effort to keep her from getting up when someone was not around, we put a guardrail on the side of the hospital bed. Mom wasn't sure she liked it until she discovered she could use it to stand up. It takes a great amount of effort for her to move from laying to sitting to standing, but then what can she do? She can't walk, so once she stands for a millisecond, she sits again, lies down, and several minutes later the pattern repeats itself. Her agitation was hard on us, and must be hard on her. We needed to be vigilant in case Mom tries to do something she thinks in her mind she can still do and falls.

According to information I read in *The Little Blue Book* from Barbara Karnes, RN, this type of continued searching for something to do, some place to go is common during the end of life.

Mom told me she was unhappy because three days ago she missed an opportunity to go through the door. As I questioned her about the door, she explained that it was the doorway to the Other Side. With unusual clarity, Mom chatted about what it meant for her. She was disappointed she missed what she felt was an invitation to let go and move along. Yet, she resisted for some inexplicable reason.

Curious to learn more about what she had seen, I asked a few questions and discovered that the door was pink. For her the door was the gateway from this earthly world to the ethereal world where she wanted to go.

The fact that the door was pink should have come as no surprise. There on her dresser Mom had already accumulated a rose quartz crystal, a round rose quartz crystal sphere, a rare pink limb rock and two pink crystal heart stones – everything we needed to create an altar next to her bed. We completed it with a continuous burning candle and a bouquet of lovely pink roses. Her pink rosary, given to her by her beloved grandmother when she was young, was already tucked under her pillow where she liked it.

The symbolism of pink crystals, the heart stone of unconditional love awakening the heart chakra was what she needed and wanted. Mom admired and approved of the altar. She loved the flowers and was specific that no cards be added.

To quell Mom's desire to roam and to allow her body and mind to calm down, the doctor recommended starting her on liquid morphine. The morphine would also help her neck muscles, which were like steel cables, to relax. If morphine gave her relief, we would all be relieved.

For this moment, Mom is in a good mood, laughing and making appropriate comments, but she is betwixt and between.

INSIGHT _____

> *Surrounding your loved one with objects, flowers, pictures, candles, and religious objects can provide comfort and serve as a ceremony or testament to the end of their life. Look around their room to see what is important to them, and if possible, place any items close to the bed. Items can also be arranged under their pillow to be felt rather than seen. Use your imagination to create something that is beautiful and meaningful.*

_____

24 HONORING YOUR ELDER

We honored Mom with an altar because that was a reflection of what she loves. Cozying her bedside table with family items, pink love stones and flowers brings her relief and recognition of her dying process. This was not maudlin or sentimental, but an honoring of her beautiful spirit. She filled her life with deep meaning through her carefully chosen art collection, books, family heirlooms and jewelry. We provided an arena for her energy to shine and be seen.

To honor Mom on another level, Sharon sang mantras, said three Hail Mary's and the Lord's Prayer. Silly us, we had to look up the words to the Hail Mary to get it right…we would start the prayer then go blank. We all giggled about this lack of Catholic memory.

Our collective honoring of Mom's dying and living went beyond the rituals. We honored her by allowing her to direct and guide us towards the end without trying to put our wants and needs in her way. By doing this, she retained control of the situation while we lovingly assisted her with quiet veneration on her journey.

AUGUST 17
Morphine

Last night we started administering a precious prescription from Mom's doctor – liquid morphine.

Mom had been so full of nervous, confused energy, not knowing where to go and what to do, and something was needed to help her relax. We hope morphine does the trick. Mom had her first dose at 6:00 pm administered by my patient husband. Since then, she slept quietly. She had lost interest in for food and occasionally took a few sips of water. Her breath was light and soft. Peace was our friend. Or so we thought. While the morphine was doing it's intended job, Mom had a new problem – deep anxiety.

Her routine had moved from quiet to a repetitious monster of getting up, down, up, down at least nine times an hour, both day and night. This activity different from the need go get up and do something of a few days ago. Now she was sitting up, then lying down, trying to change positions. Clearly she was uncomfortable and anxious.

Nancy, a relief caregiver, comes in for prayers and love, sitting by Mom's bed, supporting and recognizing the "large and small energies this soul was processing as she prepared to die."

Mom was having a lucid moment a few days ago when she was introduced to Nancy. After spending a few minutes with her, Mom said, "Thank you for coming. You are a nice girl." Our team was made of spiritually grounded people who had met with Mom's approval. This gave Mom comfort and respect along with the feeling that she's in charge of her care.

Annie, our night angel, was exhausted from Mom's circus of extreme restlessness. She suggests we ask the doctor to order Ativan for anxiety. I had heard different opinions about using both morphine and Ativan. Perhaps this will help Mom, I will let the doctor help me.

The only professional caregiver on our team, Annie, showed me an easy way to turn Mom. She put a king size pillowcase under her body as a draw sheet. I had never heard that term before, but when I saw how Annie used it to turn Mom from her right-to-left side, I was impressed. Mom was basically dead weight and no longer able to help us position her. A few bedsores are beginning to appear, so we need to change her position often. This clever technique will save our backs.

INSIGHT _____

If your loved one's actions indicate a need for medication, please do not be afraid or apprehensive to use it, especially morphine and an anxiety mixture. Morphine does not lead to a quicker death. It eases suffering and facilitates comfort. Rather than relying on the comments of well-meaning friends or the Internet, you should discuss any decision to use medication with your doctor.

_____

25 FEAR

It is now apparent that Mom is actively dying, getting very close to the end. The introduction of morphine brings relief and also trepidation. No longer can we joke with Mom, no longer can we see her smile, no longer can we engage in conversations, no longer can we relive old memories, no longer is Louie of prime interest to Mom. She is in her inner world filled with thoughts, emotions, perhaps reliving the good and odd of her life. We do not know.

Fear of the future could easily walk in the door. Each of us caregivers could get caught up in how terrible this scenario is. Yet, Mom and I have processed so much in such straightforward loving language, I do not fear. Fear can be sensed and if activated, can keep your loved one alive. They do not want you to suffer and if they sense your fear of the present or future, it may be enough to slow the passing process. It is helpful to remember the opposite of fear is love.

August 18
Plan B

The many decisions about Mom's care, especially medicine, confuse me.

All the caregivers have different ideas about how to quell Mom's anxiety and keep her comfortable. "Slow the morphine down, she doesn't need any more, she is losing her consciousness," "Change her catheter bag, she probably has a UTI (bladder infection) ..." "She needs Ativan, she doesn't need Ativan..." "We need to feed her..."

Finally, I told everyone that I would only listen to the doctor's advice. The nurse, who I unwittingly discharged yesterday thinking we did not need her services (whatever was I thinking?), sensed that she needed to check on Mom, and called to let me know she was coming by. I was extremely grateful she followed her intuition.

Agitated, Mom had a grueling late afternoon and extremely unsettled night and morning. With the nurse's help and doctor's advice, we got Mom on morphine plus Ativan.

Once her anxiety was quelled, Mom fell asleep. Now the question is, how to administer liquid medicine to someone who is sleeping? Annie knew how. She slipped her hand under Mom's pillow and raised her head just enough for Mom to swallow even though she was asleep.

A week ago, Mom said she was a bad person. Although I was curious, it was her business so I didn't ask why. It occurred to me that perhaps it is time for a priest to visit. Time for her to process what's on her mind, and get it all off of her chest, to deal with any forgiveness issues. Mom grew up Catholic with many uncles and family friends who were priests and a sister who was a nun.

When she woke up, I asked Mom if she wanted a priest to visit for confession. She nodded yes, so I called and left a message at the church. Now I worry about whether Mom will be awake when the priest arrives or if she will remember his absolution at her bedside. My soul reminds me we are energy, and even if she is not conscious, she will receive what she needs.

Since she is no longer fighting her body or mind, we expect Mom will remain in a quiet comatose state for a few days. Perhaps now that she is more relaxed and less anxious, she will be able to open and walk through her Pink Door.

Meanwhile, our time is spent loving her up. We each stop by the bed to pray or rub her back and head. Sharon sits quietly in prayer. Mo offers Mom a big smile and honors her with loving energy and more body rubs.

I hold Mom's hands and remind her of all she means to me. She does not respond, but we know she hears us and appreciates all the love in the room. There is little else to do. How much time does she have left? I am exhausted, confused and sad.

When it comes to the end of life, there are no rules, just countless options. Right now, for Mom, the process is drawn out with little visible change.

We are all waiting.

INSIGHT _____

When the energy of the one passing changes and they settle into the last days, it is time for you to change as well. Be kind to yourself as you undergo this amazing transformative process. It can be draining since there are no rules, no end in sight, and no idea of what will come next. If you can be open to being present with your loved one in the moment, you may feel a tiny bit better. When you grieve, do so out of their hearing range. They know you are suffering, and if they hear or sense your sadness, you can hold them back.

_____

26 DON'T BE SURPRISED

When your elder begins their journey to the end, they may re-embrace a religion or belief system they had as a youngster. This is a comforting and known path for them. Find out whom they desire and allow the priest, rabbi, minister, guru or whomever to come for a visit. Give them privacy to share their story, thoughts, doubts and worries with someone of their choosing. Although Mom did not attend church, she still had a deep affinity for the safety of Catholicism. It brought her relief to know she could confess. This may be the situation in your family as well.

AUGUST 19
Is Today the Day?

Mom has been quiet and peaceful since yesterday morning.

She has not had food for three days and only sips of water occasionally. She sat up for a bit, but mostly she sleeps. The meds are working to ease both her anxiety and discomfort. Her breathing is changing.

I imagine she is processing parts of her life as she prepares to cross to the other side. If she feels she was a 'bad person,' she might be reflecting on that particular incident. If she feels she could have done better in life, that could be her focus. Or, she might be enjoying all the beauty she created and the rewards she reaped by helping many others.

Of course, this is all speculation since we do not know until we are in the same space. This is a lot of work for one sweet human to do. We busy ourselves with cleaning out shelves, dusty with old memorabilia. We try not to hover. We try to be quiet, but sometimes we are unintentionally loud, causing her to startle ever so slightly.

Her bedside altar continues to grow with artifacts including more heart rocks, a written prayer and photos of her family. We shower her with love and kindness. We tell her who we imagine is waiting for her, how much we love her, and what an honor it was to either have her as a mom (John and me) or know her as a friend and teacher (caregivers). We gently stroke her with upsweeping motions to help her energy move towards her crown chakra, an energetic shift from the earth plane to the spiritual realm. Nancy and Sharon pray by Mom's side while Mo and I clean and sort. Sharon feels Mom is "sleeping and dancing with her angels," a saying Mom repeated often. It is calming to all of us to feel that the ethereal space Mom loves so much is close.

Mom's catheter leaked just a little and we are not sure what to do about it. Moving her to change sheets or remove her PJ's will only aggravate her, causing me even more anxiety. She looks so brittle, I'm afraid that moving her will hurt her. Since we did not diaper her when we could (oh my, if only she knew we were considering this dreadful act), we will let her lie in this small puddle for a few minutes until Annie arrives for her night shift. Thank goodness for Annie! Knowing how vulnerable I am, Annie gently asks me to leave the room, and sets to work. Using the draw sheet she changes Mom with ease.

Thankfully, a kind friend brought me lunch. I've been eating haphazardly for a few days. Just sitting and conversing while enjoying excellent sushi was a treat.

INSIGHT _____

> *When emotions run high and one's energy is pulled, pushed, and folded into many directions all at once, self-care is very important. Eat as best you can, rest when you can, and allow others to handle what you cannot. Know that everything is unfolding according to the universal divine plan.*

_____

27 FAMILY TREASURES

In 1985, my sister, brother and I met at our parents' beach home – no kids, no mates. Our parents, especially Mom, called us together to tag heirlooms from both sides of the family. They wanted the values both sentimental and dollar wise, to be equal. With ease, we choose what was of interest and put a sticker on furniture, objet de 'art, paintings, jewelry, valued household items and more. I was the keeper of the list.

With Mom in her last days, I checked with my family to be sure the list still represented their wishes. Thankfully, it did. We have a small family, open communication and no rancor. We agree we can trade or exchange when the time comes to distribute Mom's treasures. It is a relief to know we do not have a 'stuff-induced' emotional hurdle to overcome when Mom passes. She was wise to do this so long ago with leisurely panache. We are all grateful for her foresight.

AUGUST 20
Mom's Last Words

Annie was off duty, so I spent the night lying close enough to see and hear Mom, but far enough away so she wouldn't feel like she was bothering me, or that I was hovering.

I wonder if Mom is even breathing or if she needs me in a way I cannot not fathom.

At 7:00 am Mo came to relieve me. Fifteen minutes later, Mom was agitated. She repeated, "Mama, Mama, Mama." Mo ran to get me for help. We knew from Brian's reading (Mo was there) that Mom's mother was waiting for her on the Other Side to welcome her daughter with love and tenderness.

In an effort to soothe Mom, we reminded her of the reading, reiterating the part about her mother's love and the fact that they would be reunited. We loved her up, both physically and energetically, keeping our hands just an inch or so above her body. We knew she was relieved of an old burden of feeling neglected.

After that, Mom had a few final words. We moved the

bed away from the wall so the two of us could surround her. In a very soft voice that could only be heard if you were positioned next to her mouth, she moaned a bit and said, "Sorry, please help me. Please, please, please."

We do not know what she is sorry for, but I softly explained that God is not worried about what she did or didn't do. There is no need for guilt. She is perfect in the light and love of the Divine. Mom also said, "Clean me" and "Forgive me." These final words were of deep importance to Mom, and to me.

I believe Mom was processing her life and reliving moments in which she felt she did something wrong. We will never know, and it is none of our business. Any grief, regret, or forgiveness lives in an individual's psyche and soul. It's important to allow anything spoken by the dying to be heard without judgment. Why her body continued fighting the move to the other side is unknown. However, her words indicated she still had some things to think about or portions of her life to review.

We paid attention to her breath, her voice, her warmth, her coldness, her catheter needs, her lips, her eyes, and her essence. We held the space for her to process, to finish her business here on earth, with unconditional love.

I planted many sweet kisses on her cheek (one for each family member on the other side) and told her that I loved her. She surprised me by saying, "I love you," crisp and clear. These were Mom's last words – a deeply treasured heartfelt moment.

The rest of the day was spent with two or three people around her bed. Suddenly, I felt she might want privacy. Mo and I were filled with energy and needed a project. We focused on cleaning out her costume jewelry, which filled the dining table with no room for anything else. So

many flamboyant, colorful, crazy, unique, stylish pieces…
and, she had worn them all!

I hope Mom didn't feel our actions were rushing her
to the Pink Door. Our nervous energy had us staying busy
doing what we could to occupy our minds and keep our
sad emotions in check. All of us knew and could feel
Mom's time was getting nearer. This did not make it easy.
In fact, the realities were sinking in as Mom lay quietly
needing very little from us.

Each of us was experiencing letting Mom go from our
own perspective.

INSIGHT _____

*It's very important to honor and listen to words
spoken near the end of life. You may not know they
are the last words. If you have not said the three
most important words, I love you, now is the time. If
you have some resentment underlying your
relationship, now is the time for forgiveness in a way
that feels real to you. Your loved one may or may not
respond, but it is important for you to say what's in
your heart. This is your moment to clear the air and
bring peace to both of you.*

_____

28 FORGIVENESS

Being a neophyte at the dying process, I had no idea of the importance of forgiveness. This includes forgiveness of self, others, events and life in general for the one dying. For those remaining here on earth, it is forgiveness for whatever grievances, injustices or resentments you hold against your elder. Big stuff.

I had no need to forgive Mom. We had had a very honest and upfront relationship, and our bumps were straightened before the end. Mom's needs for forgiveness were different. They stemmed from her early childhood feeling ignored by her own mom and sad when her dad left the family.

From observing Mom, I recognized she had a need to forgive herself first and foremost for an event, a situation, a dalliance, or even her unconscious manner of putting herself down. For some reason, she felt she had been 'bad'. We did not delve into the specifics of her badness.

She had no reason to share it with me, but her Maker or God was a different story. When I had a moment to read books on death and dying, I found that forgiveness is one of the most acclaimed elements to a good death. When one forgives themselves or others, spiritual relief is found, allowing them to pass with ease in their heart and soul.

Keeping a regret or injurious pain towards someone can be poison. This is a time to let go of the energy of those old wounds and forgive yourself or others for any wrongs. The relief is palpable as anxiety is discharged, allowing for ease in passing. Does this mean you approve of any injurious actions you incurred with your elder. No, it means you love the soul they are and know they did the best they could do with their life. Judgments and resentments are recognized as you touch deeper into their soul, bypassing the ego where blame lives.

AUGUST 20
Absolution

Mom was very quiet last night. No moaning, no talking, no eating or drinking. Her time of agitation appears to be over. She is in a comatose state. Because she asked for forgiveness yesterday, I decided to call in a priest. I had actually done that on Thursday (it is now Sunday), but didn't receive a return call. In a synchronistic coincidence, Annie's stepmother had connections with the priest at our local church. She asked him to call me. After a brief phone conversation, Father Chris came right over to absolve and forgive Mom of any and all sins.

I do not believe she had any sins, but this was one of her wishes, now granted. Perhaps there was some event in her long life creating restlessness in her mind and made her feel that she needed forgiveness. Father Chris assured me that forgiveness is heard even when someone is in an unconscious state. Knowing that Mom received what she wanted brought me peace as well.

The house is changing from one of assisting Mom when she was eating, drinking, standing and walking to one of quiet loving intentional prayer and respect. Even Louie the cat keeps his distance, allowing Mom the space she needs to let go.

Mom's breathing changes as does her coloring. She goes from pink to dullness then back to pink. Her respiratory rates are all over the place – up, down, shallow, and up again, with no specific rhythm. With tenderness and devotion, Sharon prays and meditates while she rubs Mom's back and spreads lotion on her legs and arms.

Mom continues to rest peacefully with no arm or leg movements, no agitation, no pain or discomfort. We speak to her with kindness and love, knowing she can hear us. I remind her that Father Chris has been with her to absolve her sins. This is important for her to know.

INSIGHT _____

By paying attention to the daily rhythm of your elder, you can begin to understand more and more of the elements of their particular dying process. Watch and record their sleep, skin and breath fluctuations and a clear picture will begin to form. Breathe deeply and know they are doing what comes naturally for them.

_____

29 CONFESSION

Mom has had Extreme Unction (a former name for anointing the dying) and the last rites a few times. That is how close she has come to dying. This was different. This time, it was a vital request from a woman who could hardly speak and is mostly comatose. This time, it was the last time. This time with absolution, she is free to join my dad, her mom and others. Her soul, her ego and her mind are now in accord with the dying process.

AUGUST 22
Letting Go

In the morning, Annie cleaned Mom's mouth and attempted to remove her dentures but got strong resistance. She gave her a sponge bath, and dressed her in a pretty gown. Mom was ready for the day.

Mom is laboring with her breath. To quell our nerves, Mo and I continue to clean and clear out. Mom is disappearing before my eyes and it is challenging for me to watch. She is grasping for air and her heart rate is 180 beats per minute or higher. She is so thin we can see her blood racing from chamber to chamber. Her pulse is high, her color changing, she is responding quietly to touch, but just barely. She looks like a photo I have seen of her cherished grandmother towards the end of her life when she was very old, very small, and bent.

Even though she is comatose, we all treat Mom as if she is watching and hearing us. I let her know that Mo and I are putting our fidgety energy to good use, tidying up the house so it is clean. We are not pushing Mom out, just dealing with the inevitable. She is moving to a realm of the unknown where she will need only her loving soul and spirit.

Mo and I are working with earthly matters: disposable, superfluous trappings we humans collect to pretty up our lives, to make ourselves comfortable, to appeal to our senses. And Mom had a lot! We are finding items from my parent's youth, their early-married life, years of travel, and old age. The amount of stuff is overwhelming, but we sort, organize and bundle the multitude of objects into piles for thrift shops or family.

Brent and John have both been by to observe Mom's condition. Mo finishes her shift as Nancy, the visiting nurse, arrives. She is doing all the nurse things like paying particular attention to Mom's labored breathing. When Nancy gets around to replacing the catheter, we notice that Mom had her last bowel movement on the bed. This changed everything, as it was a clear indication that the end of Mom's life was very near.

With patience, Nancy directed me to move and position Mom so that she could change the sheet and clean her. One of Mom's final wishes was to be clean! Never in my wildest imagination did I picture a scene like this: I was gently and thoroughly washing Mom, almost competently and not flinching. When we were finished with Mom's clean up, Nancy swabbed her mouth and settled her on her left side. Annie had suggested placing a dying person on their left side was a way to compress the heart. After we shifted her body to her left side, her breathing started to quiet.

To continue sending loving energy to Mom, we placed her pink heart stones, crystals, and rosary on the pillow and around her head. Nancy's work was finished, and she left. Within five minutes, Mom's heart rate changed, just enough time for me to look away.

Suddenly without warning, noise, or long exhale I noticed Mom was completely still, not struggling for breath. There was no mystical experience—no vision of her soul leaving her body, no change in temperature, no lights or bells or angels. Just elegant, quiet, beautiful, tranquil peace as she desired. Her mouth was slightly ajar and her eyes were open – probably not how she imagined she would transition, yet, the sense of calm and serenity was profound. To be a witness to Mom's most tender moment as she changed from living to dying was her last gift to me.

I called my brother into the room and asked, "Do you think she is breathing?" He did not. Mom orchestrated that only my brother and I were present at the moment of her transition, allowing a healing moment for us. There is nothing like a loved one passing to open the door to forgiveness and love. My brother and I rekindled a bond we had lost. I asked him to go next door and get Brent for verification. The three of us now knew Mom was gone. She had her family with her in a circle of love. The time was 2:53PM. The three of us said our goodbyes, and then with arms around each other shed our tears.

I have heard over and over what a privilege it is to be with someone when they pass. This made no sense to me until I was with Mom in her special, final moment. All these days and years of her saying 'enough is enough' were over. She was finally free to let her spirit fly. It was an honor to witness this dynamic change from breath to no breath, from being in this world one moment to transitioning to another with silence. Birthing a newborn is breathless and marvelous, and watching someone pass on to another realm is the final circle of life, rewarding in a different heartfelt way.

I believe as Mom did that she is in her mystical home with all her family and friends. Sad as we are, we are also relieved that Mom has achieved what has been in her heart for many years. Mom finally let go and found her way with grace and quiet dignity through her Pink Door.

INSIGHT _____

When the end finally comes, it can be a time of deep relief, grief or anxiety. You will not know until you are there. If you have a religious practice, be prepared to sink into it. If not, find your way to be present for the conclusion of this very momentous occasion. If your loved one had a vision of where they would go upon dying, allow that to surface and honor it. It may not be your belief, yet it is a beautiful way to pay your deepest respect and love to them.

_____

AUGUST 22
The Aftermath

After our time of honoring Mom, it was time to call the mortuary and the doctor. The mortuary informed me that since Mom died at home, I needed to call the coroner's office first. Our town is semi-rural, so the coroner is also the sheriff. Within fifteen minutes, two fire trucks and one ambulance arrived. I had specifically requested no resuscitation since that was Mom's desire.

Why two fire trucks for a 90-pound deceased woman? When I answered the door, I was fighting mad. I would not let anyone in except one fireman who looked at Mom and declared her deceased. He asked if I had a DNR (do not resuscitate) signed by the doctor, and I retrieved the paper, which had been on her fridge for nine years. I shoved it at him and said, "Get out!!!"

I was trying so hard to protect Mom and her sweet energy from the intrusion of these men who were simply doing their job. My job was mama bear protection, and I did not give an inch. My sorrow was wrapped around letting Mom be in her peaceful sanctuary for as long as possible without intrusion.

Finally, the ambulance and one fire truck left. The

other fire personnel needed to wait for the sheriff and agreed to move the rig to the top of the drive to give us privacy. The sheriff arrived and began asking questions. He needed to talk to the doctor to determine the medical reason for Mom's death since old age is not considered a medical reason to die. I called our doctor, and she told the sheriff what he needed to hear – Mom died of heart failure. When he was leaving, I handed him all the leftover medications, as I did not want them around. They were of no use to us.

Soon after, the mortuary was cleared to come and pick up Mom. During the several hours that police vehicles, fire trucks and the coroner came and went, students were also coming and going for piano lessons from Sharon upstairs, and miraculously their paths didn't cross. The piano students had no idea what was going on downstairs. For them, it was piano practice as usual.

Sharon knew what had happened and was able to hold her emotions in until after all the students left. She was then free to grieve for the women she had watched over for so long. She had a minute between students and said this prayer for Mom:

"Oh, sweet lady, I'm so happy for you, your struggle here is over.

You've lived such a beautiful life, now YOU can fly with your angels."

When the kind mortuary men came, they asked if there were items I wanted to go with Mom (she was to be cremated). I choose the glove she wore on her left hand to keep it warm since having a mini-stoke several years ago, a toothpick (she always had one or more handy), and a rose from her bouquet (she loved roses).

Off Mom went while I went outside, sat in the sun and cried. My emotions were running high, and I was surprised at how brutal it was to see her body leaving her home for the final time.

INSIGHT _____

It is important to have paperwork in order when a loved one dies at home, including a DNR, mortuary papers, or specific paperwork needed in your state (this does not hold true when they die in a facility or a hospital). Do not call 911 unless you want the authorities to try to revive your elder. Check with your local authorities or mortuary so you are not surprised when you least expect it. Surround yourself with those who love you so you can continue to support your most precious, now-departed loved one.

_____

30 GRIEF

The death of someone you love and hold dearly can bring up a host of regrets leading to deep grief. If you have looping stories of "if only I had one more day or could say what was on my mind," that type of thinking is typically *your* issue, not necessarily the issue of the person who has passed. If you regret not saying that last significant thing to your loved one, you may become hostage to moments of unpleasant memories and unresolved grief.

Holding on to a stuck memory resulting in grief does not allow the love you carry for the one who passed to manifest. By constantly grieving, your love is overshadowed by sad emotions. Would they want you to be sad? Or would they prefer you remember a loving or a forgiving memory?

As you sit with someone who is dying, recognize if any childhood issues or buried family issues come to the surface. If not addressed, they can turn into a different level of grief. For instance, if you are still holding a grudge against your parent for something that happened when you were ten, that event may need to be explored and forgiven. You can do this verbally with the one passing, in your heart for yourself, or with a therapist. It is freeing to release long-held thoughts that could be controlling your emotions and keeping you in a grief pattern. If you say what is in your heart, both of you can have a fresh road to travel.

When a loved one is dying, you have the opportunity to express your love. Take a deep breath, look at your loved one (even if they are in a coma) and say those three magical healing words: ***I love you.*** Does that mean you need to love every minute of their life or every time you feel they wronged you? No, it means that you as a human forgive them and know they also are a human trying to make life work. This is heart and soul work. Doing this helps with grieving.

Grief, sadness, despair and heartache are necessary proponents to the death of a loved one. Everyone copes with the pain of loss in his or her own unique way. There is no special magical way or time frame to enter or exit a state of grief. Some will process their grief into a story (such as I have), some will find ways to honor their loved one with an altar or memorial, some will stay closed inside, not allowing their inner emotions to be honored. In most communities, there are grief groups where experts can help as needed.

31 LESSONS LEARNED

After Mom passed, I realized I was more than an incompetent, reluctant caregiver. I was capable of learning life lessons from Mom and others.

My limitations and impatience gave way to opportunities to soften, grow and evolve to a new levels of love and compassion. I slowed down enough to watch, process, listen, observe, relate and love the moments left with Mom rather than waste them on my usual demanding self, out of sync quick thoughts or movements. I allowed my heart to open and my tenderness to bloom. I kept a sense of humor with Mom even in the oddest of times. I appreciated the ongoing mystery of life as I witnessed her die. Mom inspired me with her attributes, values, smile and easy acceptance of all that is. She is still with me, present in her energetic rather than physical form. She is my special guide helping me when I am stuck. We chat and communicate.

I would not have it any other way.

32 SUMMARY SUGGESTIONS

- Recognize that a need for **forgiveness** usually comes into play somewhere along the line. Your loved one may need to forgive themselves or a long dead relative, or you. Don't take it personally, it is their story, which must be lifted off their chest and released.

- **Permission** to pass to the next world (or whatever their belief is) is important! Your loved one may need verbal permission not just from you, but also from other family members and friends. If anyone holds back permission, it can stop the process of dying and create unnecessary suffering.

- When expressing your **love** through actions and words – especially the all important *I love you* words there is a lasting effect on both of your spirits, bringing a sense of relief and freedom.

- By **honoring** your elder, you are graciously paying homage to the life they lived. You are allowing them to live and die on their terms, not yours.

- Be alert that the **soul/spirit** may be very anxious to depart, yet the ego/body will hold on and slow down the letting-go process.

- Be focused and **present** to the needs, desires, and wants of your loved one. This is not about you. Ask questions to start conversations like: What do you need or want, what can I do to make you more comfortable, is the music too loud, do you want me to call your sister? Stay neutral to the answers, and don't force ideas of what you think they need to do (like - you should call and talk with your sister) on them and be patient with what emerges.

- Embrace the idea that **dying is a natural process**. Allow the death process to flow and shift, as it wants to. Follow the rhythm set by the one who is dying. Try not to inflict your emotional problems onto them. Keep in mind what is happening is not about you.

- Be as **prepared** as you possibly can. Ask friends who have recently walked in your shoes for everyday practical advice. You need to create a community of helpers during this process. This may include finding a necessary hospital bed, a wheelchair, a portable potty (and other equipment), making sure you have a DNR available (if that is their desire), keeping your doctor informed, and much more.

- Search out and find excellent **caregivers**. Start conversations even with those you do not know, since you never know how you will find your necessary angels. Caregivers are angels who show up to help you. Most communities have support systems or a caregiver network set up.

- If you are the primary caregiver or the main family member**, take time** for yourself with good food, a massage, deep breathing and a walk. You cannot help when you are depleted.

I wish you and your elder comfort on your journey. Above all, be kind to yourself and all around you.

33 RESOURCES

Some of these books have been in my library for some time. Others were introduced during or after Mom's passing. This is a very small sampling. You will find just the information you need when you start your research.

Barbara Karnes - *End of Life Guideline Series.* Our go-to book, especially ***Book Three: The Eleventh Hour.*** This book gave us knowledge and wisdom we needed to deal with the very end times for Mom and what to expect.

Elizabeth Kubler-Ross – Living with Death and Dying and On Life After Death, or anything by this exceptional pioneer in the death and dying field.

Richard F. Groves and Henriette Anne Klauser – *the American Book of Living and Dying.* An American version of the Tibetan Book of the Dead.

David B Feldman, PH.D and S. Andrew Lasher, Jr, MD – *The End of Life Handbook.* A look at compassionate care.

Five Wishes – an excellent guide for Aging with Dignity and five wishes to discuss with your elder.

Robert Russo, editor – *A Healing Touch.* True stories of life, death and hospice.

Paul Kalanithi - *When Breath Becomes Air.* A young neurosurgeon dying reflects on the meaning of life and death.

I have read many books on near death experiences (NDE's), reincarnation and soul work. Here are a few

Caroline Myss – *Sacred Contracts*. Awakening Your Divine Potential. Anything by Caroline Myss.

Raymond A Moody, Jr. – *Near Death Experiences*. A classic and one of the first to report on NDE's.

Eben Alexander – *Proof of Heaven: Neurosurgeon's Journey into the Afterlife.* NDE's from a doubting doctor's view.

Betty J Eadie and Curtis Taylor – *Embraces by the Light: The Most Profound and Complete Near-Death Experience Ever*. An early classic.

Michael Newton, PH.D – *Journey of Souls: Case Studies of Life Between Lives.* This book explained so much to me. A clinical psychologist uses hypnotherapy to take clients to the other side.

George Anderson and Andrew Barone – *Walking in the Garden of Souls*. Information about the other side and advice for living here and now.

Stephen Levine – *A Year to Live.* Live now as if it were your last.

APPENDIX: MOM'S POETRY

7-26-67

Long ago
love beckoned to us
    we didn't answer
Love called
    we didn't answer
Love cried to us
    and we looked at her
    examined her
    put her away.
But love left us not
    she called and called to us
    she woke our
        icy hearts
    our untried spirits
    our passionate pride
    our secret selves
she tortured our aloneness
til finally

in full awareness of all things
    no deceit
    or sham
    or falseness
    yet mystified
      awed
we followed her in
    sadness
    sorrow
    tears, too
and we discovered she was not content
      with half measures
she demanded
    total
    complete
    subjugation
And yet thru
    tears she gives laughter
    thru sorrow she gives joy
    thru sadness she gives beauty
    and she gives us
      each other
        forever

5-10-67

The sun's rays touched the tree
    tops and me one last time
before they took this day away.
One more moment they let
their beauty linger and shine
        just for me.
And finally I let go
    for the sun must go down
    and night must come
and none but God can change
    this daily phenomena
But the beauty and loveliness
    of this day was to be etched
    in my soul for eternity

ABOUT THE AUTHOR

Suzie Daggett writes, speaks and teaches about intuition and the dynamics of soul and ego interactions. Her books offer practical life advice and timeless spiritual wisdom. Suzie is an Intuitive Business & Life Consultant.

She lives in the Sierra Nevada foothills with her husband, Brent and loves spending time with their adult children, Johnny, Kim and Anna. You will find her outside in the sunshine hiking, reading, adventuring or writing.

www.suziedaggett.com

Made in the USA
San Bernardino, CA
25 April 2018